GUIDE TO WARGAMING

STUART ASQUITH

ARGUS BOOKS

Argus Books Limited
1 Golden Square
London W1R 3AB
England

ISBN 0 85242 903 7

Phototypesetting by TNR Productions, 19 Westbourne Rd,
London N7 8AN, England
Printed and bound by LR Printing Services Limited, Manor Royal,
Crawley, West Sussex, RH10 2QN, England

DEDICATION

TO TERRY, WHO OPENED THE DOOR

"You have only to play at Little Wars three or four times to realise just what a blundering thing great war must be."

H.G. Wells, 1913

CONTENTS

ACKNOWLEDGEMENTS

The author would like to thank the many people who have
helped in the production of this book.
Particular thanks are due to Ken Jones, the Editor of
Military Modelling magazine for his continued encouragement
and support, to Rab MacWilliam of Argus Books for all his help
and to all the wargamers mentioned in the text – without their
enthusiasm for the hobby this book could not have been
written.

Unless otherwise stated, all photographs reproduced in this
book are by courtesy of *Military Modelling* magazine
photographic archives and credited where known.

1 THE BACKGROUND

Introduction

This book has been conceived and written to explain the hobby of wargaming both to the newcomer and to anyone who has ever wondered just what grown men are doing playing with toy soldiers.

So, just what is wargaming?

An oft-quoted summary by the famous writer H.G. Wells, author of the first wargames book ever published, *Little Wars* (London, 1913), bears repetition: "A game for boys from twelve years of age to one hundred and fifty and for that more intelligent sort of girl who likes boys' games and books". It is difficult to write a more apt introduction to the hobby.

A wargame can be defined as an attempt to portray a battle in miniature using model soldiers on a scaled down representation of the actual battlefield. Like all games, wargaming has rules by which to play but there is no one established set. Rather there are literally hundreds of sets commercially available and you can always write your own! This state of affairs is not as chaotic as it may appear, for as we shall see later, basic historical facts – when available – are open to varying interpretations. Also, wargames can be set in any period of history and they may range from a skirmish involving just a few figures to a major action using thousands of model soldiers.

With so many variables the reader can begin to appreciate that any one set of rules is unlikely to cover the whole range of possibilities and options open to players – wargaming really is as big as history. Indeed, if any one period of history is of particular interest to newcomers, then they are almost certain to find suitable model soldiers available in a variety of scales for that period from at least one figure manufacturer and probably from several.

A good way to start in the hobby is to follow up on a period which one has read about. In this way the requisite background information – combatant nations, theatres of war, major battles, general theme etc. – is acquired. This will act as a foundation for further research, an army and even a set of rules.

It is important to realise that wargaming is, and indeed should be, all things to all men. No one approach to a period, style or type of soldier is necessarily right or wrong. It is, after all, your time and money that are being spent on the hobby so it is important that you 'do your own thing' within the wider framework of wargaming. One of the great strengths of the hobby is that it can contain so many differing approaches and styles.

Wargaming is an expanding hobby and, although its adherents are difficult to quantify, they almost certainly number thousands in the United Kingdom and probably ten times this figure world-wide, particularly in Australia, New Zealand and North America. There is no national or worldwide overall ruling body for the hobby and, while attempts have been made at intervals to rectify this, such moves have always been actively resisted and rightly so, in the view of this author.

Wargaming is a pastime which individuals may enjoy and in which they can express themselves as they wish. To be told what to do or how to go about the hobby – the rules to use etc. – conflicts with any personal interpretations and preferences which a wargamer may have.

The Alamo under attack from Mexican infantry who are using scaling ladders to cross the walls. A wargame may re-enact anything from a small-scale skirmish to a major battle – the choice is yours.

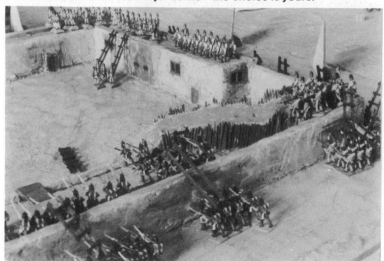

Wargamers are free to choose their own period of history, purchase those model soldiers that appeal to them and fight with those figures in a manner that reflects their personal view of the proceedings. Long may this state of affairs continue.

History of the Hobby

In hobby terms, wargaming is a relatively new pastime and three landmarks are usually quoted when tracing its history.

In the mid-19th century, *Kriegsspiel* was a regular part of the training programme of a Prussian officer. This version of wargaming was fought out on maps with the various troop types represented by suitably sized metal blocks. Although intended as a training aid for young officers, Kriegsspiel was undoubtedly fun to play and very stimulating. Possibly too, the Prussian victories against the Austrians and then France in the later 19th century attest to the games' realism and usefulness. In 1983, Bill Leeson of Hemel Hempstead re-published the 1824 version of Kriegsspiel by 1st Lieutenant Von Reisswitz and thus provided today's wargamers with a chance to test their skills at the Prussian military game.

The next milestone in the history of wargaming has already been referred to. The year 1913 saw the publication of H.G. Wells's *Little Wars* – a classic work. In this book, Wells set out the

A wargames representation of an 18th century artillery battery. The guns are deployed for action and are being manned by their crews. The limbers stand ready to take the guns out of action and in the foreground the battery ammunition wagon provides rounds for the guns to fire.

The ultimate perhaps, in wargames scenery. A German castle c1400 by Ian Weekley of 'Battlements'. (Photo I. Weekley)

basic but very workable rules by which he fought out his wargames. Using the 54mm high toy soldiers of the day, made by William Britains Limited, Wells' games required a fair amount of space. They were usually played on the floor, or on occasions the lawn, which had doubtless been mown extra closely for the event.

Then In May 1962 the book *War Games* was published, written by Donald F. Featherstone, a Southampton-based physiotherapist. This one work began the upsurge of interest in wargaming which is still in progress some 25 years later. The hobby owes an inestimable debt to Don who, with that book and his numerous subsequent titles on the subject, has probably done more for the hobby than any other single person alive today. If H.G. Wells is the grandfather of wargaming, Don Featherstone is most certainly its father.

Throughout the 1960s and 1970s the hobby blossomed as many thousands found that 'playing with toy soldiers' had gained some credence in the public eye. New figure manufacturers appeared and more books were written, with Don producing over twenty titles on the subject. A glance at the bibliography at the end of this work will reveal that the bulk of the titles listed came out in this period, chiefly in the seventies.

And so we come to the present day, where wargaming has come of age. After the two previous heady decades, the hobby is still expanding – albeit at a slower rate – but much of the

18th century cavalry canter past a village. The houses, by Games Workshop, are made from thin pre-coloured cardboard.

A corner of a wargames table showing cavalry with horse artillery in support moving through a variety of houses made from plastic and cardboard.

groundwork has been laid. New ranges of wargame figures are constantly being produced, as are sets of rules, and there appears to be a seemingly bottomless market for reference material on uniform, battles etc.

The publication of wargame or wargame-orientated books, however, has slackened off considerably and very few are still in print.

All the wargamers who might have wanted the numerous books published in the wake of the sixties and seventies 'boom' already had them and so demand gradually waned. However, nowadays there is a new generation of wargamers who are not familiar with the books published on the subject, so a new market has emerged.

Any history of wargaming, even one as brief as this, would not be complete without a mention of the Wargames Research Group. Founded in the late sixties by two experienced players, Phil Barker and Bob O'Brien, the Group, colloquially known as WRG, have produced a succession of wargame rules containing many innovations.

Seen by many wargamers as the leading light in the hobby, the WRG rules – especially those for the Ancient period – are deservedly very popular. In addition, the company produces books listing the composition of various armies covering, at the time of writing, the period 3000BC to 1700AD, and a series of quite superb reference books. The WRG have provided a great stimu-

Looking along the length of a wargames table which has been laid out for an 18th century battle. In the foreground are the cavalry and next to them is a redoubt or strong-point.

lus to the hobby and have made a lot of information easily and readily available to the wargamer.

In the 1980s the hobby is probably stronger than ever, in spite of a reasonable turnover of adherents. Age is no barrier to wargaming and it is quite often the case that, due to temporary domestic or work pressures, a player will leave the hobby to return once life settles down again. Some wargamers view the hobby as an escape from the pressures of everyday life while others enjoy the 'edge' offered by competitive games.

Ethics
Earlier in the 1980s wargaming became the target for various pacifist or anti-war groups. Conventions were picketed, members of the public who attended such meetings were harassed and generally events became somewhat silly. However, once the doubtless well-meaning campaigners were shown just what wargaming really was, as opposed to what they thought or had been told it was, events took a turn for the better and such scenes have never been repeated.

Wargaming does not leave metal widows and orphans. Areas of terrain with plastic houses are not devastated or bombarded with life-killing radiation. Rather it is a game consisting largely of skill, tempered with a degree of luck, which provides a stimulating pastime.

Before we can start wargaming we need model soldiers, an area on which to play, some terrain and various playing aids – tape measures, dice etc. – so now would be an opportune moment to look at each of these more clearly.

Model Soldiers – What are they made of?
The majority of wargames figures are made from one of two materials, metal or plastic.

The white metal used by figure producers is usually an alloy of lead and tin plus very small amounts of other metals. The proportions of each vary from manufacturer to manufacturer, the only real guide being that the more tin a figure contains the more bendable and thus less brittle it becomes. An unpainted metal figure is often referred to as a 'casting' and such figures are dangerous to very young children who may put them in their mouths. The packaging of the more responsible manufacturers carries a warning to this effect.

In the case of plastic, or more correctly polythene, figures their ability to bend is an inherent factor in the material used. Indeed such soldiers bend rather too much, causing paint to flake off at vulnerable areas such as bayonets and ankles. To a lesser degree hard plastic or polystyrene figures are also available and these usually require a modest degree of assembly – figures to fix on bases etc. – before they can be used. These do not bend as readily as their 'softer' colleagues and for this reason are popular with wargamers.

Card or paper figures are rarely seen these days although they are still produced on the Continent. Such figures, usually beautifully printed in full colour, require cutting out carefully before they can be used and are not very popular for wargames. One UK based company, Standard Games, produces a small range of such figures which can look very attractive but inevitably must be two dimensional.

Model Soldier Sizes

Model soldiers suitable for wargaming are available in a wide variety of sizes.

There is some dissension within the hobby as to exactly how the size of a figure is measured and what parameters should be used. Some designers of model soldiers opt for the soles of the figure's feet to the top of its head, excluding any hat or similar apparel. Others measure from the bottom of the figure's base to the tip of its helmet plume. The result of this is that a model soldier quoted as being, say, 25mm can in fact be anywhere between 23mm and 40mm. Although human beings are of differing sizes and statures, in the world of model soldiers such a mix of variances simply does not work out and furthermore has a tendency to offend the eye.

Also if, say, a soldier's musket was some five feet long, then

Plastic Napoleonic infantry by ESCI. These particular examples have been painted in the uniforms of some minor German states.

one would expect the scaled down version of that musket would always be of a consistent size, whatever the dimensions of the soldier. Not so. The musket, to continue our example, is depicted on the wargames figure as being of various scale lengths, grown or compressed as required to fit in with the model of its owner. This is one of the persisting oddities of the hobby – no figure manufacturer is going to change the size of his products merely to comply with those of his competitors and fellow producers. Why don't they change theirs to match his? Generally, however, the size of figures from a particular manufacturer will be constant, although this cannot be guaranteed. Only experience will tell the newcomer just whose figures are compatible with whose, but there may be some unavoidable disappointments on the way.

The sizes of model soldiers tend to be universally quoted in millimetres and this has been the case for a number of years, even before the advent of metrication. One reason for this is that the inch is rather a large unit of length for the measurements of comparatively small model soldiers. Some awkward and un-wieldy measurements can result and so the much smaller milli-metre is more suitable, convenient and accurate.

While included here for both interest and reference the scale size of a figure is rarely referred to in the wargame world. In direct contrast to the soldiers themselves, however, the model tanks, planes etc. made to accompany them are usually referred to by scale size, e.g. 1/32nd. Just for the record, 1:32 or 1/32nd means that the soldier or vehicle in question is only one thirty-second the size of the original.

In the following remarks on the various sizes of model soldiers, dimensions are quoted initially in millimetres, followed by an approximate equivalent in inches and finally by the scale size of the figures.

Some mean-looking 15mm Apaches – ideal opposition for the US cavalry of the late 19th century. (Photo Frei Korps 15)

Troopers of the US 7th cavalry ready for action. (Photo Frei Korps 15)

54mm (2¼'') 1:32 Scale This is the size of the original toy soldier, the plastic Red Indian from Woolworths, the knight in armour with a broken sword and the guardsman with his head broken off, temporary repairs being doubtless effected by a matchstick. It is also the size of toy soldiers that H.G. Wells used in his wargames. The hollow metal figures made by William Britain Ltd, plentiful at that time, are now much sought after by collectors and fetch very high prices. Their successors are nowadays all of plastic or, in the case of Britains Ltd, plastic bodies with metal bases. While perfectly good in their way these modern figures lack the charisma of their ancestors.

Should 54mm be the size of model soldier with which you wish to wargame, it is advisable to buy the plastic figures currently and readily available rather than try to obtain what are now very expensive collectors' items. There is however a marked lack of supportive material – artillery, tanks, lorries etc. – in this scale, which will cause problems.

You will see numerous advertisements from companies who produce what are termed 'traditional' toy soldiers – again these are aimed very much at the collector rather than the wargamer. While a static display of such figures looks rather splendid, they are quite expensive and costs rise sharply with such items as field guns.

Seminole Indians from Frei Korps 15. (Photo Frei Korps 15)

Another consideration with this scale is the lack of opponents. While wargaming with 54mm plastic figures has its adherents, they are very much in the minority. You are unlikely to find another wargamer in your neighbourhood with a 54mm army.

As with H.G. Wells' games, more space is required for 54mm figures but some good skirmish actions can be fought well enough. The figures themselves usually feature a wealth of detail which often repays careful painting and the variety of poses is reasonable, but the wargamer should be prepared for a fair amount of figure conversion before a balanced army can be achieved. The choice of periods is again fairly acceptable, but there is something of a bias towards World War Two amongst manufacturers of these larger figures.

30mm (1¼") 1:60 In the past this was the standard size for wargames figures. As much fine detail could be featured in this diminutive figure as on his taller and historically senior comrades and, as an additional bonus, he took up far less room. Today the 30mm soldier has for the most part disappeared but, with figure manufacturers being free in their interpretation of scale sizes, many '25mm' figures are well over 30mm.

It is rather ironic that the true scale 30mm figure will today be dwarfed by his 25mm comrades. This does have a very great advantage, however, in that the wargamer wishing to use the very limited number of 30mm figures available can generally utilise the 25mm supportive items.

Like the 54mm, the 30mm soldier can readily be used for skirmish wargames which involve only a very few figures and, again like the 54mm, it repays careful painting.

25mm (1") 1:72/76 Model soldiers of this size are very popular and have dominated the wargame world for over twenty years although recently their predominance is being challenged by their more diminutive comrades.

The variety and extent of 25mm figure ranges are extensive in both historical period and soldier type. It is probably no exaggeration to say that any model soldier you may wish to buy, irrespective of nationality, period or type, will be available from at least one of the figure manufacturers and probably from several.

In some of the more popular periods – the Napoleonic Wars for example – there is almost an embarrassment of figures from which wargamers can choose. The supportive elements too – artillery, wagons, etc. – are also very numerous.

Traditional 54mm toy soldiers: Ludhiana Sikhs by Steadfast. Such items are really for collectors rather than wargamers.

Despite competition, the 25mm figure still retains its first rank status – you will never lack for opponents with an army of this size.

20mm (¾") 1:86 The 20mm warrior is something of a curious fellow. In metal he was one of the predecessors of the 25mm size, but most wargamers preferred the larger figure and the 20mm soldier has tended to disappear. A couple of manufacturers do still produce limited ranges, however, and whenever a range of plastic figures appears on the market it is invariably 20mm in size. Be warned, though, that ranges of plastic figures are notorious for being incomplete – rarely will all types required to finish off an army be available.

The main problem is that 25mm figures really do tower above those in 20mm and the two sizes are not at all compatible. As with 30mm, restrictive figure ranges, and probably a lack of opponents, will be the chief obstacles in the path of a 20mm wargamer.

15mm (9/16") 1:120 Over the last few years, 15mm figures have taken the market by storm. Their smaller size and relative cheapness make them suitable for a goodly proportion of the wargaming fraternity. Numerous manufacturers produce extensive ranges and generally all the equipment items required are available. Such extras are much cheaper than in the larger scales and make a balanced and thus more representative army much more of an attainable ambition. One point to watch, however, is that once again figure manufacturers have put very loose interpretations on size and you will find that '15mm' actually varies between 12mm and 18mm.

Royal Naval landing party, Egypt 1882. An example of the new style 'old' toy soldier currently available. This set is by Tradition Ltd. (Photo Tradition)

With a 15mm army you are virtually guaranteed to find an opponent with a like sized army.

6mm (¼") 1:300 This size originally came into favour with the advent of miniature armoured fighting vehicles – tanks, armoured cars etc. in the same scale. The greatly increased range of modern guns and dispersion over the battlefield was difficult to re-orcate in the existing 25mm scales. The advent of 1/300 scale tanks solved this problem but even armoured vehicles need infantry support and the diminutive figures produced quickly became popular. The soldiers are available in formation blocks of various sizes or as individual figures and, while still not as well accepted as 25mm or 15mm, they are rapidly becoming so.

The 6mm soldier is usually referred to in the jargon of the hobby as 1/300th rather than 6mm – it's a strange world, wargaming.

Figure Packaging

Metal figures of 25mm and upwards are generally sold as single items, although there is an increasing tendency among manufacturers to package their figures in bags or blister packs of typically six to eight figures, or perhaps a gun and crew.

Below this, i.e. the 15mm and 6mm size, figures are almost always sold in some form of bulk packaging. Typically this would be ten infantry or five cavalry in 15mm, fifty infantry or twenty cavalry in 6mm.

Thus to a limited degree the manufacturers can dictate how many figures are bought at each time, but this does not really pose a problem and the advantages of such a system far outweigh the disadvantages.

Many more retail outlets will sell figures which they can both store and display easily. A pile of wargames figures jumbled in a box soon becomes 'bruised' and delicate items such as plumes or spear heads are easily broken – to be fair, would you buy such figures in that condition?

Plastic soldiers are usually sold in boxes of perhaps fifty figures, limiting the option of the purchaser stlll further. It is a peculiarity of plastic figure manufacturers that a percentage of the soldiers in each box are depicted in what can only be described as 'silly' poses, which are fairly useless to wargamers.

Why this state of affairs should exist has never been satisfactorily explained and, while the cost per figure is very small, the option of not having to buy such poses is not available. It is irritating not to be able to use all the figures in a box.

The presence of such silly and unusable figures in a box of plastic soldiers is one of the main drawbacks of that medium. Such poses are not found among their more suitable metal comrades.

One manufacturer of plastic figures, Peter Johnstone of Spencer Smith Miniatures, sells his 30mm troops in bags of typically thirty foot or eight cavalry figures but here, for once, all the poses are of use.

Buying Wargames Figures
Here are three ways of buying model soldiers.

First is the retail outlet, but there are precious few of these in

A WW2 German field gun, lorry and crew all produced from a plastic kit. Such items play a useful part in table top actions.

W.W. II - U.S. SOLDIERS "BIG RED ONE"

ESCI 1/72

Typical packaging for plastic soldiers suitable for wargaming, in this case for the WW2 period.

the case of metal soldiers. If you have a hobby shop near you which stocks wargames figures then you are lucky indeed and you should support the trader as much as possible with your purchases so that he will continue to stock them. The plastic figures in boxes are no problem for they are sold practically everywhere – model shops, toy shops, department stores, etc. – as indeed are the larger 54mm plastics.

The second method of buying metal figures is directly from the company which produces them. This can be achieved either by mail order or a pre-arranged visit to their trade counter if the company has one on their premises.

To buy figures through the post is a relatively simple operation. Firstly you need to decide which figures you require either by studying the company's catalogue or reading the advertisements or reviews in a hobby-related magazine such as *Military Modelling*. The company's literature – advertisement or catalogue – will tell you how much each figure or packet of figures costs and how much to add for post and packing charges – you pay for this, the manufacturer does not.

Once your 'wants' have been listed, total up the due amount, add on the post and packing – it is usually a certain percentage of the order total – and send it away to the manufacturer.

Speed of return varies enormously. Some companies deal with orders by return of post while others stipulate the turn-round period of orders in their literature. You should not really have to wait above two weeks for your figures though. If this amount of time has elapsed, ring the company to check that they have in fact received your order and if so, how it is progressing. For this reason alone, it is inadvisable to order figures from a company that does not publish a telephone number.

Alternatively you can go along to the company premises and buy figures over the counter. There are two points to watch here. Firstly such firms are often shut at weekends – the very time you are free to pay them a visit – since they are probably attending one of the many wargame conventions held all over the country. Secondly always telephone before you visit a company to arrange a mutually convenient time. Few manufacturers are large enough to permit the trade counter to be manned for normal shop hours but generally you will find that they are only too happy to accommodate you if they can.

Finally there are the wargame conventions mentioned above. These are both good news and bad news if you wish to buy figures.

The good news is the sheer number of different traders who are usually present. At the larger shows there may be up to forty or even more attending, all with stands loaded with existing, proven lines of figures or exciting new ranges.

The bad news is usually the large number of people trying to have a look at the figures and to buy some of them. You have to learn to be patient at such conventions – it always seems there is one person just where you want to be and he seems to have taken root there. Patience, patience.

What some companies will do is to bring along an order of figures for you to collect at the event. This needs to be arranged at least a week beforehand, because for the couple of days before the event, manufacturers are busy casting and loading their figures onto their van. Also the convention may be a good distance from the firm meaning that they have to set off a fair bit in advance.

Generally you will find model soldier manufacturers a friendly bunch of knowledgeable folk. We would be lost without them!

Flats

Virtually all wargame figures are fully round, i.e. three dimensional, scaled-down representations of an actual person or soldier and may be viewed from any angle.

One type of figure, however, cannot. This is the flat or two dimensional figure which can only be viewed from either side. When viewed end on, the wafer thin figures can scarcely be seen. This is deliberate, for the two sides – front and rear – of a flat figure contain a great deal of etched-on detail which repays careful painting. Indeed, some gifted people have made the painting of flats into an art form, so skilful is their work.

While they were at one time very popular on the Continent – notably in Germany – the interest in flats seems to have waned a little recently. However, several collectors will paint no other type of figure and a fair range is available from a number of manufacturers.

Flat figures are usually sold in sets of different pieces which combine with one another to produce a diorama, or study in miniature, of a particular moment in history.

The ranges of flats also contain a fair percentage of civilian subjects which obviously appeal to a wider market.

Pleasing though flat figures undoubtedly are, it has to be said that they are of little practical use to a wargamer.

Casting Your Own Figures

Another method of obtaining wargame figures is to cast your own from commercially available moulds. At the time of writing the only company offering such moulds are Prince August, based in Ireland.

What happens is that you buy a mould, ladle and metal from the company. The metal is melted down in the ladle over a heat source and when suitably molten poured into the prepared mould. After waiting for the metal to cool, the two halves of the mould are separated and the casting gently removed.

A home-made mould in silicone rubber used for casting 19th century artillery pieces in low-melt metal.

Such a method is not without its benefits but it is fraught with potential dangers. Heat and molten metal are very dangerous items and should always be treated with the utmost respect. It is possible to make your own moulds, but in my view this is even more hazardous and for that reason will not be discussed in this book.

Beware of one thing – it is illegal to buy a commercial figure and use it as a master to make a mould in order to cast more of the same figure. Not just wrong – illegal. Should you be found 'pirating', as this is called, the company whose figures you are using can take you to court. Such infringements of copyright are often vigorously pursued, so be warned.

Conversions

It is the way of the world that no matter how many wargame figures are available, there comes a time when you have need for a figure of a particular type of soldier that you cannot buy. This state of affairs heralds the need for an available figure to be altered or converted into the different style of soldier required.

Conversions can take many forms. The simplest type is simply a painting job – the figure is repainted in a different colour of uniform to achieve the desired effect. Thus a French Napoleonic line infantryman meant to have a basically blue coat can become a Saxon (white coat) or Swiss (red coat) infantryman of the same period. An American Civil War infantryman in a kepi can be used to represent a Mecklinburg-Schwerin infantryman of the Austro-Prussian War (1866), a Wurttenberg infantryman of the Franco-Prussian War (1870-71) or a Greek infantry private of the Balkans Wars (1912-13) in much the same manner, and so the list goes on.

The next stage is to swap the heads of figures. This is a little costly, for two figures are needed to produce the one conversion, but this is a small price to pay for just the right figure for your wargames army.

The arms of figures can be carefully bent into new shapes – usually only once in the case of metal figures for they may snap off if this is tried too often. Any weapon the figure holds can be removed by cutting it away and a new one fixed in its place. By this method, a figure armed with a halberd can be re-equipped with perhaps a sword and shield.

Similarly, officers waving swords and pointing – normally in the direction of the enemy – can be altered to be infantry flag bearers or cavalry standard bearers. The sword is removed and the hand

The end result of home casting. Cleaned up and painted, these Napoleonic light cavalry are ideal for wargaming.

re-shaped or carefully drilled to accept the flag pole with the colour attached. As an alternative the sword can be retained and the pointing hand used to grip the pole. Just how a cavalry officer controls his mount after such attention is open to debate, but such figures look splendid on the wargames table as they lead their units in the charge.

Complete figures can be cut or sawn in half and new tops or bottoms added as required. Horses can be given similar treatment to produce new poses or style.

The only limitations are the converter's own imagination and acquired skill. While the opening remarks in this section may imply conversions are born out of necessity, many wargamers convert their figures simply to make them more individualistic and unique.

This is fine and deserves encouragement, but one word of caution. To convert one figure is fun, to convert a few is not too bad, but to have to convert a regiment of say twenty figures can be tedious in the extreme, unless the conversion involves only a paint job.

Conversion Techniques Metal figures are no more difficult to convert than plastic ones, but each possesses contrasting properties and demands a slightly different approach and technique.

Generally speaking metal figures need to be either filed or cut with a fine saw rather than with a knife, for it is highly likely a knife blade will snap under the required pressure. Parts can be fixed with suitable glues – epoxy, contact adhesives and super glues (cyano-acrylates). These last named can be very dangerous to use for they bond skin in seconds and should always be treated with the utmost respect. If you can avoid using them you are wise

A part scratch-built ammunition wagon or caisson. The horses and wheels are plastic items, but the body of the wagon has been constructed from balsa wood.

to do so, at least until you become relatively adept at conversion work.

Gaps can occur when a joint is created or remade and these can be filled with *Milliput* or similar epoxy putties. When dry such fillers are very tough and can be sanded down to blend in with the rest of the figure smoothly.

Plastic figures are best tackled with a modelling scalpel or sharp pen-knife, clean decisive cuts being essential. Sawing or indeed filing motions on soft plastic figures produce masses of fibres which have to be cut away – a laborious job.

Heat can be used to some effect for converting plastic figures – immersion in hot water for a brief period can make a figure soft enough to bend into a new position in which it remains after removal from the water. Similarly the heated tip of a needle (held safely by a clothes peg or cork handle) or knife will be found to seal joints on plastic figures very well after a bit of practice.

One additional problem with soft plastic figures is that none of the glues mentioned above are very successful with them. The contact adhesives are about the best but it will be found that re-fixed arms or heads, for example, need the extra support and strength of a pin pushed through them and into the main body of the figure.

Hard plastic (polystyrene) figures can be treated in much the same way as soft ones, but one thing in their favour is that brush-on or tube-applied polystyrene adhesives or cement (the type used for plastic model kits) will work well on them, making conversions that little bit easier.

General Points When converting figures it is important to work both tidily and safely.

Keep all the figures and parts on a work surface with a raised edge on three sides to retain all the small pieces. A tray is also useful for keeping items safe and preventing them falling onto the carpet and halting the conversion whilst the wargamer and any available members of the family crawl round on hands and knees looking a figure head some 8mm big.

If you are using the kitchen table make sure you protect the surface before you begin. A newspaper opened out is useful and a cutting or work board is easily obtained by buying a suitable off-cut of chipboard, say 24 × 12 × ⅝in.

Before you start work on the figure lay out all the glues and tools you will need to prevent frenzied dashes out to the shed or garage for a pair of pliers of whatever, just as you have the conversion nicely under way.

You will need a few fine files – usually referred to as needle or Swiss files – some small finely pointed pliers, tweezers, sand or emery paper, a small hobby saw, perhaps a hand driven pin drill, a modelling scalpel, a pen-knife, a clothes peg (very useful for holding parts in place) plus any other odds and ends. Experience will tell you what you will need and a simple tool kit will give you an inexpensive basis on which to build, although the above list should cover most eventualities.

A selection of glues will be needed. Look after these, for they are fairly expensive and can be messy if left to their own devices. Like most things, glues are harmful if used wrongly – always read the manufacturers' instructions before using them.

Also, before you start ensure the lighting where you are working is adequate and then have a quiet moment's thought about just what you are going to try to achieve. Sketch out some ideas as although not all of us are artists, a couple of drawings or pictorial references of the intended result to hand are very useful. Finally, take care. You will be using sharp tools and effective glues and fingers are more important than toy soldiers.

In this short section I cannot hope to have explained the art of figure conversion fully and the foregoing is only a very general-ised outline. I would recommend the following books as further reading on this fascinating aspect of the hobby: P. Blum, *Model Soldiers* (A&AP 1971); R. Dilley, *Scale Model Soldiers* (Almark 1972); S. Goodenough, *Military Miniatures* (Orbis 1977); P. Stearns, *How to make Model Soldiers* (Hamlyn 1974); M. Windrow & G. Embleton, *Model Soldiers* (Airfix Magazine Guide, PSL 1976).

Painting

If a book could be written on the conversion of figures, then a whole series could be based on the subject of wargame figure painting.

In my opinion, by far the best paint to use for wargame figures is the range of matt finish plastic enamels produced by Humbrol Ltd. The selection, availability and usefulness of the range make them ideal for the wargamer. There are other paints, of course – smaller ranges of plastic enamels by Revell, for example, oil paints, water colours, poster colours, acrylics etc. However, Humbrol is still the clear market leader. Plastic enamels require the paintbrushes you are using to be cleaned in white spirit, so have a small screwtopped bottle of this to hand, along with a piece of kitchen roll or cloth on which to wipe and clean your brush.

Brushes Paintbrushes are very much a matter of personal preference.

The best idea is to buy the very best quality brushes that you can afford, and your local art shop or model shop should stock several ranges at varying prices. Modern nylon brushes are quite good, as are squirrel hair etc. Whichever type of brush you buy, look after it and preserve its point. Clean it well each time

Essential requirements for painting. Good brushes safely stored and a cleaning agent – white spirit in the case of the popular enamel paints.

you use another colour and at the end of the painting session. Store the brush in an old mug or similar container so that it can be kept vertical – bristles uppermost. Some shops sell brushes with a plastic bristle guard; keep this and it can be slipped back over the brush after use each time.

Brushes come in many sizes but you will find sizes 0, 1 and perhaps 2 suitable for most painting jobs. As your new brushes begin to wear use them for gloss varnishing and undercoating, keeping your newer brushes for more delicate and detailed work.

Preparation Do not rush home with your newly acquired wargames figures and immediately begin to slap paint on them – some essential preparation is necessary first.

Plastic figures are generally sold in boxes and when the box is opened it will be seen that the figures are connected by at least two points to some lengths of sprue. This is the plastic which has cooled outside the mould which formed the figure. The soldiers need to be carefully removed from it by using a sharp knife. Once free of the sprue, the figures will have a slightly 'greasy' feel to them and will need swishing around in a bowl of washing up water and wiping over with a cloth.

They should be dried and then checked for any stray pieces of plastic which might be clinging to armpits or under haversacks etc. Any such pieces should be carefully removed with a sharp knife – as ever, take care.

The individual soldiers can then be fixed onto temporary bases in order to facilitate painting without the figures themselves being handled. Beermats cut into 1 × 1 in. squares make very suitable bases for 20mm figures and contact adhesives such as *Evo-Stik Clear* will secure soldier to beermat quite satisfactorily. Once the glue has set, usually after a couple of hours or so, the figure is ready for painting.

Metal figures generally do not need washing, although there is a school of thought among wargamers that they do benefit from such treatment. Close attention needs to be paid to the figure to remove any pieces of 'flash' or surplus metal. Sometimes this can be removed with a pen-knife – rarely with a scalpel, for the blade will undoubtedly break – and sometimes with a file.

Once cleaned up the metal figure, like his plastic comrade, needs a base on which to be fixed for painting to avoid handling. Here beermats will not do the job. Plastic figures snap off beermats easily and cleanly – metal ones do not as the adhesive

Not a wargame but an exciting large diorama by Ted Surèn using 30mm figures to illustrate the battle of Tankondibo. Now in the Museum of Military Miniatures in Tangiers.

sticks better to the metal and the mat tears into layers and has to be cleaned off the base with a pen-knife. Very messy.

Thick plastic card and shiny-faced cardboard are useful for this job, but not balsa wood as it will splinter and break as the figure is removed.

So we have our figure, metal or plastic, on a temporary base. The next step is to apply an undercoat in order to provide a surface on which to paint. While plastic figures can be painted without an undercoat, the colours do not show nearly so well, and on untreated metal figures they are positively drab.

An undercoat is a thin coat of matt white or perhaps light grey which is brushed over the entire figure, so sealing its surface completely. It is important to ensure that the undercoat is fairly thin otherwise some of the detail on the figure may be obscured. Some wargamers prefer to undercoat using an aerosol spray can of paint. A couple of points are important here. Firstly, it is advisable to spray your figures within the confines of, say, an empty grocery box in order to contain the spray of paint. Secondly, the figures must be checked thoroughly several times to ensure that all their surfaces have been covered. Whichever method is used, the figure should then be left to dry at least for a few hours and preferably overnight.

Now the painting proper can begin.

Plastic enamel paint can separate in the tin and will often need a good stir for about half a minute or so before use. Yellows, oranges and reds are particularly prone to this but it is a good idea to get into the habit of stirring all colours before you paint with them. If you don't, the part you do use will dry shiny or thin and the remainder of the tin will become thick and go hard, rendering it unusable. Only by stirring will you obtain the colour the manufacturers intended. Once you have stirred the contents of the tin, use a wooden cocktail stick or something similar to lift a quantity onto a suitable palette – a tin lid, plastic lid or piece of card. Always put the lid firmly back on the tin each time. Carry out your painting from the amount on the palette – if you need more, add from the tin. If you paint directly from the tin, its top edges will become encrusted with dried paint, the lid will not shut properly and the contents will solidify.

Opinions on what to paint first on a figure are divided. Some wargamers paint the face first, some the main colour – usually the coat – whilst some work from the 'inside outwards', i.e. the lowest surface, typically trousers, first then the next and so on. The best method is the one that suits you but beware of painting adjacent areas before the paint on one of them is dry, otherwise they may blend and run.

Again, experience will decide what is best for you but wargamers rarely paint one figure at a time. This is both time-consuming and wasteful on paint – don't forget the figures are being painted in order that they can be used in a game. While it is enjoyable enough in itself, painting for a wargamer is only a means to an end.

To paint between ten and twenty figures at once will be found to suit most wargamers on average. What happens with this method is that all the figures have, say, their coats painted. Once this is done, the painter returns to the first figure and then paints, say, the trousers on each figure. The idea is that in the time it has taken to paint all the figures, the first figure's colour has dried and thus another colour can be applied.

This need not apply only to uniformed troops, however. Native or barbarian units with variously coloured clothing can still be painted in much the same way. Select a colour – say dark grey – and paint the trousers of the first three figures in the line. Then take perhaps a blue and paint the tunics of the second and third figures plus the fourth in line. Thus the method is basically the same, but the application a little different by being staggered, for undisciplined troops were rarely uniformed.

This process is repeated along the line until the figures are completed – or almost.

How far the painting goes depends on the required finish for the figure. Wargame figures can either be left matt – the colours once dry being protected by a coat of matt varnish – or given a coat of gloss varnish. This does impart an unreal or 'toy soldier' finish to the figure but the colours do appear that bit brighter and the figures are pleasing to handle. The choice is entirely up to the wargamer. If the figure is going to be varnished – and it is advisable to do so, otherwise the paint will show fingermarks and eventually come off with the constant handling wargame figures suffer – this should be done before any metallic colours, gold, silver etc. are applied.

If such colours are painted on prior to varnishing, they will simply lift off as the varnish covers them and will spread onto the other colours – again messy. So take your figures up to the metallic stage, varnish them and then, once the varnish has dried (usually overnight) add the gold or silver as required.

You will find that modern wargame figures have a good amount of detail and will repay careful painting. There should

These 54mm Knights are large for grand-scale wargames but can be used for small actions and are rewarding to paint. Part of castle wall is an attractive accessory, made by 'Battlements'.

English Civil War figures can also be colourful. The 'Battlements' Tudor house is more elaborate than strictly necessary for wargaming, but many wargamers also enjoy modelling.

however be a limit to the detail painted in, otherwise you will be painting forever and not wargaming.

Paint in facial detail if you wish – eyes etc, shade the figure, outline the crossbelts or whatever with a fine black line, the choice is entirely yours. Some wargamers have turned painting of figures into an art form and this is fine, but not essential.

The figures are needed for a game, so paint them to the best of your ability but don't let the tail wag the dog. The aim is to have painted units on the wargames table, not a dozen unusable masterpieces on the shelf to show for a year's work! On the other hand try not to be too impatient or slapdash – soldiers have to be reasonably dressed in order to fight well! Do not worry if your painting does not initially come up to your hoped-for standard – you will improve.

For this reason, resist painting guard or elite units straight away. Paint up some rank and file units first and then as your painting improves (and it surely will) tackle the guard formations.

As far as mounted figures are concerned, have a good look at horses and see just what colours and shades these animals are. It is useful to have a colour reference book on horses to hand, a cheap children's one will suffice just so long as it features colour plates or photographs of the various breeds. Try to reflect these colours when you paint the animal. Similarly, if you are painting a camel unit, take the family to the zoo and study camels closely and then try to match up the colours you have seen.

There are arguments for and against gluing the rider in place before you paint him or painting the man and his mount separately. As ever, whichever method suits you best is the one to adopt.

With plastic figures the paint will almost certainly come off certain areas – bayonets, swords etc. This is unavoidable and is due to the flexibility of the plastic rather than to any poor workmanship on your part. All you can realistically do is check your plastic figures every so often and touch up where the paint has flaked off.

Professionally Painted Armies You will see numerous advertisements in publications such as *Military Modelling* placed by companies prepared to paint your wargames figures for you. If you do not have the ability or time to paint your own figures (think carefully, you probably have both) then professional figure painters are there to help.

Usually such firms consist of one person painting at weekends or evenings as he works through college or perhaps to supplement the family budget. Some companies however are quite large concerns and employ a number of painters to tackle the work. Some will paint the figures you provide, others quote prices which also includes the cost of the figure itself.

The painted figures are sent to you completely finished – gloss or matt varnish as requested – and can at once be placed directly on the wargames table. The time taken with your order will depend very much on the quantity involved, the size of the company and the amount of work they already have in hand, but we are probably talking in terms of weeks rather than months.

Other companies offer ready-painted units or armies for you to buy off the shelf, rather than your own specified figures or regiments.

Both types of company offer a fairly high quality product and seem to be growing in popularity.

The figures produced are, of course, relatively expensive. Any prices quoted here will doubtless be well out of date by the time you are reading this. To offer some guide, however, profession-ally painted figures generally cost between four and six times the amount of the casting itself. This makes units and armies quite expensive – indeed some companies offer credit terms to facili-tate payment – but you do receive in return a well-painted body of figures, ready for instant action.

Apart from this financial aspect, however, when someone admires a particular unit it is a bit disappointing not to be able to

Renaissance period Russian troops from Essex Miniatures show a variety of figures and weapons giving painting scope.

say that you painted them. There is a danger, too, that you will not have a 'feel' for the figures in the same way in which you would have had you painted them yourself. If neither of these points worry you, however, you will find that most figure painting companies offer a high quality and reliable service, relieving the wargamer of the imagined drudgery of painting armies.

Figure Basing

Few wargames figures these days feature large enough bases to permit them to stand up on the wargames table. Usually the base is the minimum area required to fix the figure's feet to and thus renders the soldier top heavy and prone to falling over.

Most sets of wargame rules set out the base sizes of various types of troops – light infantry, heavy cavalry etc. The sizes stipulated do vary to a certain extent from one set of rules to another but a degree of standardisation is now beginning to arrive. Typically the rules call for an individual infantryman to be set on a 20 × 20mm base.

What material can we use for a base? First on the list are beermats and, since the figures are not going to be removed from the bases, these will serve equally well for plastic or metal figures. Readily available and easy to work, beermats do not warp and are fairly rugged.

Thin plywood is also ideal, if somewhat more expensive. Plastic card is not too good as its shiny undersurface will often let figures slide backwards down any hill slopes they may be asked to climb in the course of a wargame. Reasonably thick card, e.g. from shop display signs, is also useful but be careful it is not too thin, for it will warp and not support the figure on it.

The minimum work required is to glue the fully painted figure on to a base pre-cut to the required size, paint the base a suitable colour and that's that. There is nothing wrong with this but, should the wargamer wish, the appearance of the base can be improved both to complement the figure and to add that finishing touch.

Dark Ages figures with different weapons mounted as individuals or pairs, which helps with casualty accounting!

Several methods can be used to achieve this and all require the figure to be firmly glued on the base first. Try painting the base with a suitable gloss paint. Immediately the base is painted, immerse it in a box of model railway scenic flock. The flock will adhere to the paint – remove the figure, shake off any excess flock and put to one side to dry. Some flock will fall off but, because you have used gloss paint which is thicker than matt, it will have a better chance of retaining the flock on the figure's base.

Another method is to coat the base carefully – again with the figure fixed in place first – with a filler such as *Tetrion* or *Polyfilla*. Once the material has dried and hardened off it can be painted in matt colours and looks fine. A couple of problems, though – such fillers will crack and chunks will break off during a game. This is both annoying and visually irritating for, where the filler has broken off, areas of stark white will be revealed which somehow seem to emphasise the event.

A third method is to buy some cage-bird sand from your local pet shop – a bag costing well under £1 will be sufficient for an entire army – and some white glue, such as *Evo-Stik Wood Adhesive Resin 'W'*. Put a small amount of glue onto a suitable surface, preferably with a rim or lip – typically a plastic lid – and gradually stir in some sand until a fairly loose but gritty paste results. Carefully apply this mixture to the figure's base using an old table knife. Take care not to get the stuff on the figure's legs but, if you do, leave it, as it is easier to remove when dry.

Then, when you have covered the base, immerse it in a box or tray of the sand in much the same way as flocking, shake gently and set aside to dry. The glue hardens off leaving a rather pleasing rough surface which can be painted. One word of warning, though. When painting over such a base use an old brush, for sand will pull the bristles out and generally chew up the brush. While the base is still wet, it can be further decorated with lichen, again available from model railway shops, or short (½in.) lengths of sisal string to represent coarse grass.

Up to now we have considered a single man on a single base. If you have a wargames army of say 250 to 300 figures, to move each one individually may be judged to be tedious in the extreme. To avoid this, units are often put on multiple bases to lessen the time spent actually moving the soldiers around the table top.

Since most rules allow for some unfortunate figures to become casualties in a battle, you cannot really put, say, a twenty man unit all on one common base. Some rules however do allow for this, so be careful to check the rules you intend to use before fixing figures on multiple bases. One exception is the 6mm troop block where numerous figures are actually cast onto a unit base.

A compromise solution is best, and the diagram below gives an indication of a twenty man unit based for ease of movement and yet with sufficient single bases to permit removal of casualties.

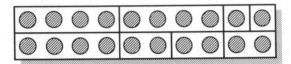

A schematic view of a wargames infantry unit illustrating the use of multiple basing for figures.

Thus if three figures become casualties a strip of two plus a single would be removed. If then another man fell, these would be returned and a strip of four figures removed, and so on.

The individual base sizes of the figures are still retained under this system – for example the base with four figures on it would measure 80mm long by 20mm deep if each figure has the 20 × 20mm base size mentioned earlier.

Note that four figures is the maximum number on any one base. More than this will cause the base to sag under the weight of the figures. Generally speaking beermats only measure 100mm or less anyway, which limits them to set maximum number of figures.

Some figures have larger bases. Those of light cavalry, for example, usually cover quite an area to represent the open formations in which such troops fought. Here units are smaller anyway and it may be found to be convenient simply to base the cavalry in pairs rather than larger multiples, leaving a couple of singles, again for casualties.

Many wargamers, even though they multiple-base the bulk of their army, prefer to leave their light troops – foot and horse – on single bases in order that they can more easily fulfil their role in the wargame.

As mentioned previously, most rules now agree on base sizes but, as a general guide, always check the sizes stipulated in the particular set of rules which you intend to use before basing your figures. Re-basing is a messy and tedious business.

WARGAME UNITS

Figure Ratios Assume for a moment that the historical unit that you wish to recreate for a wargame had a strength of a thousand soldiers. Now clearly you cannot represent such a formation with a thousand wargames figures. The cost involved would be extremely high and the space necessary to accommodate such a unit considerable. Bear in mind also that that is only one unit and you are going to need several, and in addition perhaps some for the opposition as well.

The way wargamers work is to adopt a ratio between the actual historical organisation and its wargame counterpart. Thus if one wargames figure is taken to represent a hundred real figures, our thousand strong unit would be represented by ten wargame figures – you see the idea?

Various figure ratios are popular and some of them are listed below.

	Ratio						
Unit Size of	1:1000	1:100	1:50	1:40	1:33	1:20	1:10
1000 Men	5 figures	10	20	25	30	50	100

Which ratio is selected, and you can of course choose your own, will depend very much on the playing area you have available, storage space and financial limitations. Further, the size of the wargames figure will affect the ratio chosen. Clearly the 6mm figure will allow a much smaller ratio than the 30mm figure. A scaled down unit of 30 figures in 6mm may be judged rather too small to be representative of an actual unit, while in 25mm it is just about right.

A good deal of thought has to go into which ratio to use, for once you have made the choice you must stick with it for all the parts of your wargames army. Thus if you have opted for, say, a 1:100 ratio which looks good for infantry, it may look rather odd having to have one mounted figure purporting to represent a hundred strong cavalry formation. The vital factor here is consistency – it must be stressed that the same figure ratio must be used throughout your army.

One or two problems are often met when trying to scale down the supportive arms – typically with artillery.

The basic organisational unit of the artillery was the battery, usually of six guns. This is virtually impossible to scale down so one alternative is to consider the number of gunners serving the battery. Let us assume for a moment that there are 140 gunners in our imaginary battery, a fairly typical number.

Unit Size of	1:200	1:100	1:50	1:40	1:33	1:20	1:10
140 Men	—	1	3	4	4	7	14

Thus had you adopted a figure ratio of 1:200 for the infantry you would now be faced with a real problem for the artillery.

Say the 1:40 ratio is used – remember it must be the same for all three arms of your army, infantry, cavalry and artillery – then four gunners would be grouped around a model field gun to represent the battery for wargames purposes.

Higher Organisations Much will depend on the period you choose and the nationality of the army. While there are numerous similarities, not all countries organised their forces in the same way so you will need to establish some basic information before you start to plan your wargames army in any detail.

A typical layout of an army is shown in the diagram below. It is very generalised but will serve to show the relationship between the various formations.

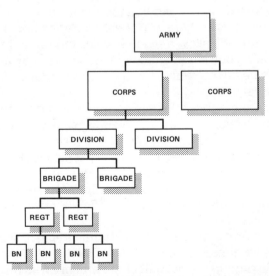

A generalised and simplified organisational breakdown of a typical Army.

Regt. = Regiment   BN = Battalion

Historical Examples Establish the basic strengths of the units you wish to recreate, decide on a figure ratio and off you go.

Some examples may help – a Roman cohort of the 1st Century AD was 480 strong, a Prussian regiment of foot during the Seven Years War (1756-63) was 1700 men strong, a British Napoleonic heavy dragoon regiment had 900 troopers and an American Civil War regiment of infantry was 500 strong. So it goes on – apply your chosen figure ratio to any of these actual historical strengths and you have the strength of your wargames unit.

Some types of unit defy scaling down – a medieval siege train, for example, or a Marlburian pontoon and bridging train. Here you simply have to use your common sense. It is no good having an infantry unit of say six figures if your siege train is composed of thirty model cannon.

Study your period carefully and try to obtain an idea of just how big such types of unit were and apply a sensible ratio. Generally speaking, between one and three wagons will make up a quite satisfactory pontoon train and perhaps up to four heavy guns plus their attendant paraphernalia will represent a siege train well enough.

Frontage Ratios An alternative way to scale down units for the wargames table is to consider the actual frontage occupied by that formation. For example, if a Seven Years' War Prussian infantry battalion has a frontage of 125 yards, then this distance is scaled down and the number of wargame figures who can fit in this frontage is the size of the unit. For example, say that one inch on the wargame table represents one yard in real life. Thus the frontage of our wargames unit would be in the order of 125ins. – pretty extensive.

This however can be reduced to produce a more manageable and workable distance. Take one inch as representing ten yards this time and now we have a wargames frontage of 12½ins. which is perhaps somewhere in the right region. Obviously the scale of the figures will govern just how many of them make up the unit – there will be more 15mm than 30mm for example – but the general principle should be clear from the above.

These ideas can also be applied to cavalry and artillery, but here not only the frontage but the depth of units also needs to be considered – did they deploy two, three, four or more ranks deep on the battlefield? Again this needs to be amended until visually pleasing, but it will be generally found that wargame units deployed in one or two ranks look about right.

Points Values Once units of troops have been amassed there is a need to balance armies between opposing sides or players.

One method is to allot say 50 cavalry, 200 infantry and two guns per side. This is fine, but does not take into consideration the differing types of soldier involved. For instance, if all the infantry in one army are heavily armed and armoured men-at-arms, and their opposition consists of peasants armed with sticks, it is hardly a fair fight.

An alternative is to allot a points value to each type of figure or unit of figures. For example our men-at-arms in the last example would have a basic value of one point plus five for armour, another five for a shield and perhaps a further five for a weapon – sword, mace or whatever. Thus the points value of such a figure would be 16. The peasant on the other hand would only have the basic value of 1. So, the peasant commander should have 16 figures for every man-at-arms on the table.

Some rules suggest points value for figures, but you can also allocate your own. The WRG Army Lists mentioned earlier work on this points basis as they offer guidance on putting an army together.

Playing Area The majority of wargamers play on the dining room table or a similar temporary playing surface. Only a few are fortunate enough to have their own permanent wargames table. Your available playing area is one of the factors to consider when selecting the size of wargames figures as well as the figure ratio. The average dining table measures perhaps 5′ × 3′ and as such offers a reasonably sized area. For many years all the present writer's wargames were played on the dining room table and great fun they were too. Providing the consent of the presiding domestic authority is obtained, wargames can be quite happily played on such a table. It is unwise to plan anything too ambitious, however, since the rest of the family will also lay claim to the table, even for such relatively unimportant things as eating!

Two wallpaper pasting tables side by side make a fairly useful playing area, but they do need covering, otherwise there is inevitably quite a wide gap between them. A board laid on your bed is OK but has two drawbacks – move on the bed and the board will tilt, reducing your fine army to something of an ignominious heap, and when you go to bed the playing area has to be stored somewhere. A board with folding legs which hinges against the wall is another idea, but it takes up a lot of wall space in the 'up' position.

A prepared artillery
position, cast in
resin and suitable
for post-1914
actions.

Really, the playing area you have available will to a large extent be dictated by your domestic arrangements.

The floor is not a realistic proposition, in spite of earlier remarks relating to the games played by H.G. Wells. Knees soon become sore, figures get trodden on, the family pet becomes a real menace and general fatigue sets in fairly quickly.

One day you may well aspire to your own room, but never be despondent if this remains an unattainable ambition. The fun in wargaming is the enjoyment it brings you, not the size of your table.

Scenery and Terrain So far we have our model soldiers about to manoeuvre over a plain playing area. We know the countryside is not like this whatever the place and time, so how can we create some sort of scenery on our wargames table?

The first need is probably for hills, rivers and roads. To look at hills first, these can be achieved by books placed under a

Tank traps were important obstacles in World War 2. Those in the photograph are cast in resin.

A wargame in progress over an uncluttered terrain. Note the effective use of items of terrain to produce an open playing area.

suitably coloured cloth or by shaped polystyrene ceiling tiles or carpet tiles piled on top of one another until the desired height or arrangement is achieved. Some companies produce ready-made hills but these tend to be expensive.

Remember, your soldiers will, generally speaking, have to stand on these hills so the stepped or layered method is a good one to use.

Roads and rivers are basically the same except the former are painted brown and the latter blue. Pieces of card can be used in sections say 2-3ins. wide and perhaps 6-8ins. long. Bends and curves should also be made in order that your roads and rivers tend to appear more natural.

Next come trees and buildings. While you can make your own trees, commercially available ones are so good and relatively cheap that it's not worth the effort. Have a good look round your local model shop and do not forget to check out any model railway shops too – they very often have scenic items which are useful to wargamers.

More than any other scenic item buildings set the time and place of the battle. You would not expect to see a thatched cottage on Ancients wargame tables, nor perhaps a Greek Temple decorating an English Civil War battle. Relate your buildings to the period and scale you have chosen and they will complement your figures well. Choose a basic stock of say half a dozen buildings and they will stand you in good stead for many

Pubs can feature in wargames! 'La Belle Alliance' was not far from the action in the Battle of Waterloo, a favourite choice of many wargaming clubs and groups.

years. Such buildings can be scratch built without too much difficulty, but are also commercially available in cardboard, plaster, resin and plastic.

Just as we used a real to wargame figure ratio, so we use a real to wargame scenery relationship. One house represents a hamlet, two a village, four a small town and so on. Likewise one tree is a copse, a couple a small wood, a dozen or so a virtual forest. Only experience and your available playing area will decide which is right for you.

An American Civil War railway loading dock modelled to 15mm size and cast in resin by Gallia.

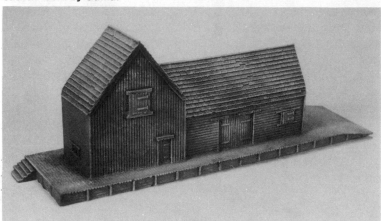

A contrasting style of terrain complete with well modelled buildings, fields, roads etc. Such objects can however restrict the actual playing area.

As to other items, ploughed fields can be represented by varyingly coloured squares of felt, inexpensively obtained from wool shops or handicraft shops. Fencing, hedges and walls are widely available commercially as are items such as bridges, castles and churches.

Do not spend too much money initially on your scenery. After all you might not stay with your first choice of period and – dare it be said – you might not even stay with the hobby.

Many commercially available items of scenery are expensive, so only buy them if you are sure. The money spent on, say, a commercial model of a 25mm castle would have bought you an awful lot of wargame figures, so take care before you buy.

Good terrain will complement your wargame figures and make the battle look just that bit more meaningful and realistic. Scenery may also provide tactical objectives for a wargame, where such items as crossroads take on an importance all of their own.

Dice and Tape Measures To introduce a certain degree of luck or chance into a wargame – war is after all an art not a science – dice are used. The use of dice in a wargame does not reduce it to the level of *Snakes and Ladders* but serves to introduce the random element of battle.

There are many types of dice, the most familiar of which is the six sided cube carrying a series of dots or pips ranging from one to six. This is the most popular and oft used die in wargaming, but there are others. Sometimes the range of numbers possible on the one to six die is too large for a particular set of rules.

A useful alternative in this case is the 'average die', again six sided but carrying the numbers 2, 3, 3, 4, 4, 5 on its sides. Thus, the possible range of numbers which can be obtained is reduced both by removing the one and the six and doubling the occurrence of the middle order numbers three and four.

Some 'regular' dice also use numbers in the place of pips and thus show the full 1-6 range, so take care when buying dice to ensure that you select the ones you actually want.

In addition to the usual six sided dice – whatever their markings – there are numerous other shapes and sizes. Four sided pyramid shaped, eight sided, ten sided, twelve sided and twenty sided are all readily available and all have their different uses. Generally it is within the realms of fantasy wargames that such dice are employed, but since they do exist and offer varying ranges of numbers, they have potential use in all wargaming.

A bag of paper chits with numbers on them and a printed set of random numbers are also alternative methods of offering chance results, but dice are much easier to use and are both readily available and very cheap to buy. (Incidentally, a *die* is correct but modern usage seems to be 'a dice' so we will use this.)

During the course of any wargame, distances either for movement or ranges have to be measured. By far the best device for this is the handyman's retractable metal tape measure – the sort that pulls out from a small squarish box and will lock in place, but which snaps back in once a button or whatever is pressed. While on the expensive side, one of these will provide you with years of wargaming measurement. There are other methods of course – an ordinary 12in. ruler in wood or plastic will suffice as will a linen tape measure or a home-made measuring stick.

Some wargame rules require measurements to be made in inches whilst others call for millimetres, so it is a good idea to ensure that whichever ruler or measure you use is calibrated in both these scales.

THE WARGAME

Scaling Down The sizes of wargame units have been scaled down from their historical counterparts, and it is equally necessary to make some adjustment to unit capability. A wargame move is purported to represent a set amount of time, a minute for example, and everything a real soldier could achieve in this period of time can also be performed by its model equivalent. Assume a soldier could fire his bow four times or his musket once or cover 100 yards of ground or whatever – all these activities must be scaled down.

For this, two parameters are used – time scale and the ground scale. It may be a minute, perhaps two, perhaps only thirty seconds, but the time scale chosen must remain constant throughout the rules. Let us continue our example and say that this period of time allows our early 19th century soldier to fire his musket once or advance 100 yards. Now some idea of the distances involved is necessary and here is where the ground scale comes into things.

Let us assume for the moment that 1in. in our wargame represents a real yard. Thus our man, able to cover 100 yards in a minute, would also be able to cover 100ins. in a wargame. Using the same scale, the ball fired from his musket with an average range of say 400 yards would cover 400ins. However, the above example creates distances which are rather too large for war-

Character can be introduced by well-modelled buildings and scenery. This is the thatched hospital hut which featured in the Zulu attack at Rorke's Drift.

Cavalry charging a defended small building in a colourful scene. Note the assorted bases which make casualty accounting simpler.

game purposes. To underline this take the case of artillery in the same period with ranges of typically 1,000 yards – giving a scale range of 1,000ins. or 83 feet.

Two popular and workable ground scales are 1 in. equals ten yards or 1 mm equals one yard. Thus 100 yards will be scaled to 10ins. in the former or 100mm in the latter, which is more suitable. Again there is nothing to stop wargamers using their own ground scales but always remember, be consistent.

The Conduct of a Wargame A wargame is split into a set or unspecified number of turns or moves. Each turn can be said to be sub-divided into phases or sub-sections which follow the same sequence: Movement, Firing, Melee, Morale.

The movement section or phase permits the players either simultaneously or alternately, dependent on choice or the rules in use, to move those of their soldiers that they wish to in accordance with the distances specified by the rules. In the firing phase all troops capable of firing, and desired to do so by the players, may fire – again, method, ranges and effect will all be covered by the rules. Casualties are removed and the turn moves on to the melee phase. In this section any hand to hand combats, termed 'melees', are resolved and again casualties removed. Finally comes a morale check.

A well organised and neatly presented demonstration wargame in progress at a Convention.

To explain this last item, morale is the imagined mental state of your model soldiers in the wargame. A regiment of cavalry thunders across the wargames table straight at a unit of enemy infantry – will the infantry stand firm or will they run? Morale will decide. Various conditions are assessed; the unit's experience, efficiency, status, etc. which, with the consideration of a dice roll to represent the imponderable factor, will decide the reaction of the unit in question. Should the infantry break and run the cavalry will in all probability cut them down. If, however, they stand and fire then the cavalry themselves will have to have their morale checked to see if they still charge home on the infantry.

This completes the turn and the game moves on to the next one. As mentioned, wargames can be of a set length, e.g. one side has to capture a village in say 12 moves or the game carries on until either side has clearly won or the time comes to stop playing.

Casualties In the section which dealt with the basing of wargames figures, we saw that some figures could be on individual bases in order to facilitate their removal as casualties. Not all rules require the removal of figures to indicate the casualties that a particular unit has suffered, but it is safe to say that most do.

There are two main schools of thought on casualty representation in wargames.

Firstly there is the 'one man equals one figure' approach. In this, if a unit suffers say six casualties, then six wargame figures are physically removed from that unit on the table top.

When one considers, however, that under an earlier heading we saw how one wargames figure can represent a variable number of real soldiers, this one-to-one casualty system seems to offer something of a paradox. In point of fact, it doesn't, for the rules allow for the fact that one figure does indeed represent a number of actual men.

Against this method is the slight imbalance it seems to represent when viewed against the background of wargame units being scaled down representations of actual units, rather than on a one-to-one basis. Strongly in its favour however is the fact that no paperwork or book-keeping is necessary.

The second approach is to remember that one figure does indeed represent a number of men. Casualties inflicted on a unit are recorded on paper and when the number of casualties suffered by a unit exceeds the figure scale, then one figure is removed. An example may serve to clarify this method.

Say that in a Napoleonic period wargame, a unit of Austrian infantry, 30 figures strong, represents an actual infantry battalion of 960 men. Thus each wargames figure stands for 32 actual soldiers. As the unit suffers casualties, these are noted on paper in a cumulative total. Thus if the unit received say five casualties on move 1, ten on move 2 and three on move 3, the record would run:

Move:	1	2	3
Casualties:	5	15	18

This method continues until 32 is reached – once it is, a figure is removed from the wargame unit and any excess casualties carried forward.

Move:	3	4	5	6	7
Casualties:	18	24	31	44*	12

*Figure removed, thus 44 − 32 = 12, therefore 12 casualties are carried forward.

This approach maintains the figure's ratio, but does involve some records being kept. This is not necessarily an arduous task however and many wargamers feel the end result is worth the effort involved.

In simple terms the actual casualties are inflicted by the enemy, either by long range fire (artillery etc.) or shorter range fire (archery, musketry) or melee (close quarter weapons).

Factors such as range and defences are considered. As ever a dice is introduced as a variable and the resultant figure is the casualties inflicted. Again, an example might help.

Say a unit of 40 wargame archers wish to fire at a body of enemy foot soldiers. Under the imaginary set of rules in use we find that archers have one dice per 10 figures firing thrown for them. Thus the player with the archers rolls four dice: assume 3, 4, 2 and 6 result, so that means that 15 potential casualties are caused. However, other factors can come into play – if the target unit was behind cover, for example, it is reasonable to expect that they would suffer fewer casualties than one stood out in the open. Also, if that unit was composed of heavily-armoured men with shields they in turn would suffer less than lightly-clad villagers.

The range at which the firing takes place is also relevant – the nearer the firers are to their target, the greater chance they have of hitting that target. One can only generalise here – the various

A most useful item of wargames equipment, a horse-drawn wagon. This example made by Gallia.

rules themselves will explain the specific systems adopted by their author to reflect firing etc.

Wargame units seldom fight on to the last man, or rather figure. The rules will decide, but generally continuing casualty losses will have an adverse effect on the morale of a unit and may cause them to either give ground or run away. The effectiveness of a unit suffering heavy casualties will also be reduced and thus may cause that unit to be withdrawn from the firing line or combat by the controlling player.

Winners and Losers The outcome of a game can sometimes be difficult to assess but basically there are three methods of determining which side has won.

Firstly the players can agree that the wargame will last for a set number of moves. When the last move has ended – unless, of course, there is an obvious and clear-cut result prior to this – both sides can assess to what degree their tactical aims have been achieved, and how many men they have lost. The winner is the one who has most of the former and least of the latter.

Another method is to give one player an objective, when if this is achieved that player wins the game, if not then the other player wins.

Finally there is the fight to the finish, where the game carries on until one side concedes defeat.

All these methods have points for and against them and wargamers are free to adopt any or none of them as local circumstances dictate.

How many Players? The maximum number of players able to participate in a wargame is usually set by the physical limits of

Home produced items of wargame scenery. Here fir cones have been used as trees and the bridge is constructed from paper and cardboard.

the playing area. Clearly a hundred players could not all congregate usefully around a 6 × 4ft. wargames table. Generally two, three or four players will be found about right for most games. Wargamers however are not totally dependent on others for a game and solo wargaming is a most absorbing aspect of the hobby, with many adherents either from necessity or choice.

Wargame Rules Wargame rules will reflect most if not all the foregoing points and will offer to the player a complete package with which to conduct a wargame.

The many sets of commercial rules vary in complexity, content and presentation. Which set is chosen will be very much a matter of personal choice. Whatever may be heard to the contrary, no set of commercial rules enjoys universal acclaim, but some are admittedly more popular than others.

When you first start wargaming it is advisable to avoid the more complex sets of rules. This is not a condemnation of them, for complex rule sets are perfectly acceptable and provide quite reasonable games eventually. It is just that their sheer complexity will undoubtedly overawe the beginner and in all probability deter him or her from wargaming.

A simple set of rules will be a far better introduction to the hobby, but as always this remains very much a matter of personal taste and choice.

As mentioned previously, wargamers can write their own rules and they can even be published if one has the necessary contacts. Many wargame clubs either use their own rules or heavily doctored versions of commercially available sets. As a general rule it is better to start with a simple set, to get the 'feel' of them and then progress if required to the relatively complex sets.

One point worth making is that just because a set of rules is complex – 'comprehensive' is the label usually attached to such works by their author(s) – it does not necessarily mean that it is better than a relatively simple set.

Apart from all the important criteria of personal preference, there are other points to consider when considering wargame rules. Does the wargame seem to 'flow' along, are the tactics of the period encouraged, are mistakes by generals going to be punished, are they easy to absorb? These are all questions which need to be answered by the rules themselves to the satisfaction of the wargamer intending to use them.

Written Orders Units need orders on which to act during each move or turn of the wargame. These are normally written out on an order sheet. The orders can be as complex or as brief as required, indeed simple symbols, such as arrows to show the direction in which a unit should move, can be utilised.

Some sets of rules allow for writing of fresh orders in every wargame move whilst others insist given orders must stand for a specified number of moves, typically three. There are varying schools of thought on this aspect of the game. Written orders for every move offer the players an almost god-like control over their units, something a real general could never have had.

However, if orders are deemed to stand for a set number of moves, then there is always the human tendency to 'amend' those intended moves to suit what the opposition are doing. Orders for each individual turn do prevent one side from instantly reacting to the manoeuvres of the other side and allow some degree of surprise to be possible.

These houses are scratch-built from balsa and complement any wargames table.

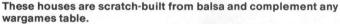

In any event, written order sheets act as memory aids for the players. When moving perhaps 20 or 30 units on the wargames table, players can genuinely forget what they had intended to do with a particular unit, so the order sheet comes in handy.

Also if your opponent brings off a particularly dazzling manoeuvre which completely confounds your operational plan, you can ask to see the order sheet to check that the moves were pre-planned.

Finally the order sheet is the place where a unit's casualties are recorded, if the wargames rules in use employ this method.

Summary
So far we have seen something of the history of wargaming and have examined the figures used – sizes, organising, painting and basing. The playing area, terrain and other items necessary for a game – dice, order sheets etc. – have all been covered.

It is now time to look at the various historical periods available to the wargamer, along with an outline of what each of the periods has to offer. Before we do this, however, a few general points of explanation regarding the rules you will find in Section 2 of this book may be in order.

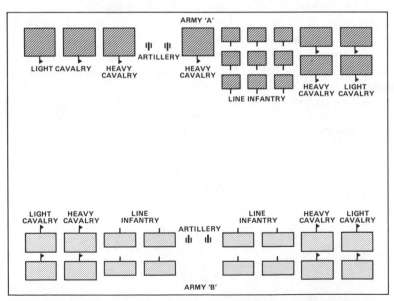

Two wargames armies laid out at the start of a game. Very often the terrain will govern initial deployment and variations are practically endless.

These rules assume that a wargame terrain has been set up and that the various units of troop types of the period chosen have been laid out on it.

Both armies are usually deployed relatively near their own edge of the wargames table in an array thought suitable by the players.

If a specific battle or scenario is being fought, the initial deployment may well be radically different, depending on the action to be re-fought.

It is from this initial 'free' deployment that the rules which are set out on the next few pages will come into use.

The rules will give the distance a soldier or unit can move each wargame turn, how far he can fire etc. and will generally control the game.

Moves or turns by the armies involved in a wargame can be either simultaneous – which is preferable – or alternate between the two opposing forces.

Basically, after initial deployment, both players decide on their respective plans of action. Then on move one, any or all of their units may be moved in accordance with the distances stipulated by the rules. Once this has been completed, any firing or hand to hand combat (melee) is resolved and casualties – if any – removed or noted. The game then moves on to move two and the process is repeated.

Finally, a few definitions to help clarify the rules which follow in Section 2.

Movement This is the maximum distance which a troop type can cover in one wargame move. The actual distance covered can vary as required and indeed the figures can remain stationary if the controlling player so desires.

Some terrain obstacles can affect movement – generally units on hills move at half speed, as do troops fording rivers. The move restriction lasts as long as any part of that unit is in contact with the obstacle.

If a unit rotates completely around or through a right angle then it may only move at half speed during that turn in which it carried out the manoeuvre. Lastly any troops firing while moving (note crossbowmen cannot do this) have their maximum moves reduced by half.

Dice Throughout these rules, the dice in use are the standard six sided type, with faces numbered 1–6.

Dice Modifiers The dice modifiers to the firing and melee rules apply to both sides, thus each group in a melee can have, for example, the benefit of +2 on each die thrown for them.

Melee This is the physical combat part of the move. To be eligible to take part in a melee, figures have to be in base contact. The maximum odds permissible in a melee are 2:1. Thus, two foot figures can fight one, or one cavalry figure can fight one foot figure. If a third figure should be available, then he is barred from taking part in the melee until such time as one of his comrades falls. Then he can take his place, making his presence felt on the subsequent move.

Rallying This is the re-organising after a melee part of the game. Units rallying may not move – apart from dressing ranks etc. – and may not fire or melee. If they are fired on they suffer normal casualties and if melee'd cannot defend themselves.

Elephant and Chariot Casualties It is a good plan to allot defence values to elephants and chariots. When they suffer casualties, the casualty score is deducted from the defence value. When this value reaches nil, the elephant or chariot is removed from the table. Pieces that have reducing defence values need not be removed from the board. Suggested defence values are 15 for an elephant and 10 for a chariot – light or heavy variety.

One elaboration could be that elephants suffering casualties to over half their defence value will run amok in a direction decided perhaps by a pencil spun on the table top. They will plunge off in this direction, scattering friend and foe alike as they go. Once the elephant reaches the table edge, it is removed and takes no further part in the game.

Flags, Standards One suggestion to add an extra degree of excitement to a melee is to allow the winner to throw an extra dice after the outcome has been decided. Should this dice come up as a six, then the flag, standard or emblem of the opposing unit has been captured and must be handed over. It may be re-captured in the same manner.

One elaboration on this is to subtract one from all dice thrown for the unit which has lost its flag, but this may be somewhat harsh.

Defences The rules here are intended for field actions rather than sieges but on occasion field works are constructed and defended in battle.

Troops attacking such defences are −1 on all dice thrown for them to represent the additional protection offered to the defenders by those field works. All troops behind defences suffer only half the standard casualty rate.

Artillery Movement The move distances for artillery refer to a piece being man-handled in action. Out of battle, the gun would be hitched to a limber or gun tractor, depending on the period, but this is not covered in the rules. Note that a gun may not move and fire in the same turn.

Flank or Rear Attacks Units attacked in the flank or rear are at a distinct disadvantage. Thus a unit attacked in the flank is −1 on all dice thrown, and −3 if attacked from the rear.

Heavy, Medium and Light These adjectives are applied to some troop types and some weapon types in the following rules. The definition alters with the various periods, but the aim is to provide the wargamer with the chance to divide his forces into appropriate types, if required. ·

World War One Onwards Inevitably, the reader will judge the suggested rules for WW1, WW2 and the Modern periods to be somewhat oversimplified.

As the nature of warfare becomes more complex, so must the rules for wargaming. Only land warfare is covered and then only in a very general sense. Ground attacks by aircraft, naval bombardment, surface to air missiles and even hand grenades have been omitted in the interest of brevity and simplicity. As ever the reader is free to add suitable rules and build on the basic ideas to produce a more comprehensive set.

2 THE RULES

Which Period do I Choose?

The choice of wargame period is as wide as history itself. For wargaming purposes the eras of history are usually placed into convenient headings which will be discussed here.

The coverage of each section may vary slightly, but all the following will be dealt with in a similar manner: the combatant nations with their 'years of power', the various wars and their major battles, a general outline as to the period's wargaming potential, some generalised and simplistic playing rules and finally a short bibliography for further reading. This last named will by necessity vary in length, for some periods of history are longer than others whilst others again are better documented. Readily available, easy-reading titles have been selected in favour of rare works which are hard to obtain.

The Ancient Period

Generally regarded by wargamers as covering the years 3000BC to 500AD, the Ancient period covers history from its origins and encompasses all the armies and peoples of the ancient and biblical worlds.

To attempt to summarise in a couple of paragraphs what amounts to well over half the world's documented history is clearly nonsensical. Instead, a rapid survey of the major nations of the period must suffice to whet the appetite of the newcomer.

The Achamenid Persians (500–300BC) Due to the victories of Cyrus the Great, the Achamenian Persians by 500BC held military sway over an empire reaching, at its greatest extent, from the Danube to the Indus rivers and from the Caucasus to Egypt. Their main opponents were the Greeks, whom they fought on land and sea, but it was the Macedonians led by Alexander the Great who brought about their downfall.

An Ancient wargame in progress. The defenders are about to sally forth against their attackers.

Most readers will probably have heard of Thermopylae (480BC) where a few Greeks from Sparta held a huge Persian army under Darius. Other major battles included Kunaxa (401 BC), Marathon (490BC) and Plataeae (479BC).

The Ancient Britons (55BC–500AD) Invaded in 55BC, 54BC and 43AD by the Romans, the British tribes offered a mixed resistance to Roman rule. The only major battles were at the Medway in 43AD and when the queen of the Iceni tribe, Boudicca, led an unsuccessful revolt against the Romans in 61AD. Operating with 'kick and rush' tactics and placing reliance on light wickerwork chariots – long in disuse on the continent of Europe – the British were no real match for the Roman Legions.

The Assyrians (1100–612BC) The Assyrians ruled over all the known world during the specified years, maintaining large and efficient armies.

The horse-drawn heavy war chariot came into use at this time as did armoured – as opposed to the previously lightly-clad – cavalry. Another speciality of the Assyrians was the storming of cities and fortresses for which they had many specialised devices. Their main opponents were the Babylonians, Egyptians and Persians but it was the Medes who finally overthrew the Assyrians themselves.

The Carthaginians Carthage was a North African state which fought three wars with Rome on land and sea. These conflicts, referred to as the Punic Wars, were dated 264–241BC, 219–202BC and 149–146BC. Their famous general Hannibal won a series of notable victories over the Romans but ultimately the might of Rome destroyed the power of Carthage for good, razing the city to the ground.

Major battles: Cannae (216BC), Ilipa (206BC), Lake Trasimene (217BC), Trebbia (218BC) and Zama (202BC).

The Egyptians (3000–1100BC) The first major military race to appear was the Egyptians, one of the world's oldest civilisations, whose history is usually divided into three kingdoms – Old, Middle and New. The Egyptians' chief opponents were the Hittites, Libyans, Syrians and the Sea Peoples. The best known action is probably Kadesh (1288BC) where Pharaoh Rameses II fought an indecisive action against the Hittites.

The Greeks (600–300BC) The mainstay of the Greek army was the foot soldier, initially heavily armoured and equipped with a long spear and shield. Referred to as a 'hoplite', the soldier was a Greek citizen whose wars were nearly all waged against other Greeks. The chief city states of Greece – Athens, Corinth, Sparta and Thebes – were constantly fighting one another, but they did band together to defeat the Persians.

The Greek states remained geographically small and formed only temporary alliances with one another. Many Greek soldiers became mercenaries both in the armies of other city states and indeed in the armed forces of other countries.

The Huns (350–450AD) The Huns were a fierce race of natural horsemen who, after defeating the Goths, advanced westwards from their homes in Eastern Europe. Their most famous leader was Attila and under him the swiftly moving army of horse archers and light cavalry swept all before them until halted in 451AD at the battle of Chalons-sur-Marne by the joint command of Romans and Visigoths.

The Macedonians (350–150BC) The Macedonians are well known for the campaigns of Alexander the Great who inherited a superb army from his father King Philip. At the battle of Issus (333BC) Alexander overcame the Persians and ended their period of power.

The Romans (200BC–400AD) The Roman Empire was founded after numerous wars which can only be noted here.

The Punic Wars was a struggle against the great sea power of Carthage, while the Gallic wars saw the conquest of much of North West Europe. Indeed, Rome fought at one time or another on all her frontiers, both while they were being established and afterwards, and had a wide array of enemies.

Major battles include Cannae (216BC), Cynoscephalae (197BC), Pydna (168BC), Teutoburger (9AD) and Zama (202BC).

The foregoing can really only scratch the surface of such a long period. The most popular wargaming nations have been noted but space precludes the mention of many more races – Arabs, Babylonians, Celts, Chinese, Gauls, Etruscans, Hittites, Jews, Mongols, Nubians, Parthians, Philistines, Phoenicians, Phrygians, Picts, Samnites, Sassanid Persians, Scythians, Seleucids, Semites and so on. The Ancient period is indeed rich in choice for wargamers.

Simple Wargame Rules for the Ancient Period

Movement: Light Infantry 9″   (Units may move and fire)
Heavy Infantry 6″
Light Cavalry/Camelry 15″
Heavy Cavalry/Camelry 9″
Light Chariot 12″
Heavy Chariot 9″
Elephants 6″

Firing: One dice per 10 figures able to fire
Maximum ranges Spear 6″
               Sling 12″
               Bow 18″
Score on dice is the number of casualties inflicted, subject to the following cumulative amendments:
Firing while moving −1
Firing at over half range −1 from each dice score
Firing at armoured or shielded troops −1 from each dice score.

Melee: Either (A) single combat, one dice per figure, highest score wins; or
(B) One dice per 10 figures able to fight, dice score gives casualties inflicted.
Either method is subject to the following cumulative amendments:

Mounted troops fighting troops on foot, +1 to each dice thrown for mounted troops.
Fighting troops with shield or armour, −1 to attackers' dice.
Two figures fighting one figure, +1 to each dice thrown for the two figures.
Completely unarmoured troops, −1 to each dice thrown for them.

At the end of a melee count up the casualties. The side with most − all units involved go back one move at the maximum speed for their type and spend the next move rallying. The winning side spends the next move after the melee rallying on the site of the melee and can then act as their general wishes. If the first round of a melee ends in a draw a second round is fought during the next game move. Melees can only last for two consecutive moves after which, if there is no clear outcome, both sides move back a full move and spend the subsequent one rallying. Both sides are then once again capable of action.

Suggested Reading

Barker P., *The Armies & Enemies of Imperial Rome 150BC–600AD* (WRG, 1972)

Buttery A., *Armies and Enemies of Ancient Egypt and Assyria 3200BC–612BC* (WRG, 1974)

Connolly P., *The Roman Army* (MacDonald, 1975)

Greer J., *The Armies & Enemies of Ancient China 1027BC–1286AD* (WRG, 1975)

Head D., *Armies of the Macedonian & Punic Wars 359BC–146BC* (WRG, 1982)

Nelson R., *Armies of the Greek & Persian Wars* (WRG, 1975)

Saxtorph N., *Warriors & Weapons of Early Times* (Blandford, 1972)

Simkins M., *The Roman Army from Caesar to Trojan* (Osprey, 1984)

Simkins M., *The Roman Army from Hadrian to Constantine* (Osprey, 1979)

Stillman N. & Tallis N., *Armies of the Ancient Near East 3000BC–539BC* (WRG, 1984)

Warry J., *Warfare in the Classical World* (Salamander, 1980)

Wilcox P., *Rome's Enemies (2): Gallic & British Celts* (Osprey, 1985)

Wilcox P., *Rome's Enemies (3): Parthians & Sassanid Persians* (Osprey, 1986)

Wise T., *Ancient Armies of the Middle East* (Osprey, 1981)

Wise T., *Armies of the Carthaginian Wars 265–146BC* (Osprey, 1982)

The Dark Age/Feudal Periods

The Dark Ages are usually referred to as the years 500–1000AD, whilst the Feudal period is considered to cover 1000–1200AD.

The Dark Ages saw the end of the Roman Empire, the advent of the Vikings and several invasions of the British Isles by Angles, Jutes and Saxons. Much of the history of Britain in the Dark Ages is taken up with the various conflicts caused by the Saxons and their allies establishing a hold over much of southern and central England. It is at this time that King Arthur, leader of the Romano–British, emerges as a champion against the invaders.

The Saxons themselves had problems with the Vikings, who were raiding Western Europe and the British Isles during this period, and indeed by the 10th century had colonised virtually all of Britain apart from Wessex which was ably defended by Alfred the Great.

Another tribe of raiders, land-based this time and called Magyars, ranged at will across France, Germany and Italy, to be finally stopped by a German army under Otto I at Lechfeld (955).

The Carolingians had an empire from 814–887AD. Established by their famous leader Charlemagne, the empire covered most of Europe but was split by internal dissension. A Viking assault on Paris in 886AD saw its final collapse.

The Visigoths controlled Spain along with a portion of Southern France and frequently clashed with the Burgundians and Franks who entered France from the East.

The Vandals were active in the Mediterranean and Africa but

Dark Age infantry in 25mm. The lord of the manor looks on from behind the main infantry line.

were in turn destroyed by Byzantines who were themselves a strong force in this period and ruled over a large empire.

The Holy Roman Empire, initially consisting of Burgundy, Italy and Germany, was founded in 887 and immediately launched into a period of intensive warfare against France, Bavaria, Bohemia and Italy.

In Eastern Europe the Bulgars increased in power and during this period Croatia, Poland, Russia and Serbia were all engaged in wars, both internal and external.

In Asia the Sassanid Persians also had an empire and clashed with the later Roman forces in a series of campaigns. Arabia, Abyssinia, China, India, Japan and Korea were also all active during this period.

Major battles of the Dark Age period include Brunanburgh (937), Cotyaeum (493), Melitene (576), Mount Badon (517), Salona (536), Taginae (552), Tricameron (534) and Viminacium (601).

Turning now to the ensuing Feudal Period (1000–1200AD) we find some familiar names – Richard the Lionheart, Saladin, William the Conqueror, King Harold and Hereward the Wake.

The crossbow made its appearance, polearms became more fearsome and there was a tendency to favour infantrymen rather than the dominant mounted soldier.

In 1066 Harold Hardraade invaded Northern England and established a hold. King Harold marched north to defeat him, only to have to turn around, retrace his steps and face a second and larger invasion led by William of Normandy. Harold fell at the Battle of Hastings and England came under Norman rule. Hereward the Wake led a sustained rebellion against William but this ended when the Normans stormed Hereward's stronghold. The rule of England passed through several kings in this period ending with Richard I who spent most of his time away on Crusades to the Holy Land.

The period also saw the continuation of border wars between England and Scotland, with incursions carried out by both sides. Also contesting territory, France continually tried to restore her control over the country and recover the English possessions there.

Spain too saw its share of fighting with the slow process of Christian reconquest continuing in the face of severe Moslem opposition.

The Byzantines were still very much in evidence but their

empire was finally brought to an end by the Seljuk Turks at the end of the 12th Century.

The Crusades The Crusades were essentially military expeditions mounted by Western Europeans for religious reasons – to wrest the Holy Land from Moslem control – but politics also came into play.

There were three main crusades, 1098–1102, 1147–1149 and 1189–1192 respectively. In the final analysis little was actually achieved, for frequently both sides were split by internal disputes. Further, the Moslem leader, Saladin, was a talented general and not until his death in 1193 were the Crusaders able to hold ground.

One development of the expeditions was the establishment of several military orders of monks such as the Knight Templars, the Knights of St. John (or Knights Hospitallers) and the Teutonic Knights. Such orders provided a secure base in the Holy Land, building huge castles and offering 'on-site' trained bodies of reliable fighting men.

Major battles of the Feudal period include Antioch (1119), Arsouf (1191), Fulford (1066), Hastings (1066), Manzikert (1071), Northallerton (1138), Philomelion (1116) and Stamford Bridge (1066).

Simple Wargame Rules for the Dark Age and Feudal Periods

Movement: Light Infantry 9"   (Units may move and fire)
Heavy Infantry 6"
Light Cavalry 12"
Heavy Cavalry 9"

Firing: Spear 6"   One dice per 10 figures able to fire.
Sling 12"
Bow 18"
Crossbow 18"
(N.B. crossbowmen cannot move and fire in the same turn)
Score on the dice is the number of casualties inflicted, subject to the following cumulative amendments:
Firing at over half range −1 from each dice score
Firing at armoured or shielded troops −1 from each dice score.
Firing and moving −1

Melee: Either (A) single combat, one dice per figure, highest wins. This system is strongly recommended to re-

Some Eastern troop types suitable for the Ancient or Feudal periods by Essex Miniatures.

flect the style of fighting which dominated the greater part of these periods.

(B) One dice per 10 figures able to fight, dice score gives casualties inflicted.

Either method is subject to the following cumulative amendments:

Mounted troops fighting troops on foot, +1 to each dice thrown for mounted troops.

Fighting troops that have shield or armour, −1 to attackers' dice.

Two figures fighting one figure, +1 to each dice thrown for the two figures.

Completely unarmoured troops, −1 to each dice thrown for them.

At the end of a melee count up casualties. The side with most – all units involved go back one move at the maximum speed for their type and spend the next move rallying. The winning side spends the next move after the melee rallying on the site of the melee and can then act as their general wishes. If the first round of the melee ends in a draw a second round is fought during the next game move. Melees can only last for two consecutive moves after which, if there is no clear outcome, both sides move back a full move and spend the subsequent one rallying. Both sides are then once again capable of action.

Suggested Reading

Garmonsway G. (trans.), *The Anglo Saxon Chronicle* (Dent, 1972)
Heath I., *Armies of the Dark Ages 600–1066* (WRG, 1976)
Heath I., *Armies and Enemies of the Crusades 1096–1291* (WRG, 1978)
Heath I., *Armies of Feudal Europe 1066–1300* (WRG, 1977)
Nicolle D., *Arthur & the Anglo Saxon Wars* (Osprey, 1984)
Wise T., *Armies of the Crusades* (Osprey, 1978)
Wise T., *Saxon, Viking & Norman* (Osprey, 1979)
Wise T., *The Knights of Christ* (Osprey, 1984)
Wise T., *The Wars of the Crusades* (Osprey, 1978)
Wise T., *1066 Year of Destiny* (Osprey, 1979)
Wood M., *In Search of the Dark Ages* (BBC, 1981)

The Medieval Period (1200–1480)

The medieval period saw alterations both in the use of armour and in the style. Previously any armour that had been worn was of mail, iron rings linked together. As the period progressed, mail gave way to plate armour which was so effective in protecting its wearer that a shield was no longer needed. Instead of ordinary horses, mounted men at arms clad in full plate armour needed sturdy cart-horse type mounts to carry the resulting weight. Lighter types of horsemen did exist, but the Medieval period is essentially about the armoured knight on horseback.

A new infantry weapon was the longbow which in the hands of a trained man could deliver a frighteningly accurate shot several times a minute – ordinary bows or crossbows were overwhelmed by this weapon.

Another innovation was the arrival of gunpowder on the battle-field. Initially used for unreliable artillery pieces, gunpowder increased in presence as the period went on, with infantry being armed with a primitive form of rifle towards the end of the 15th century.

The early part of the period saw the Mongols under their leader Genghis Khan sweep all before them in Eastern Europe and Asia. Among many conquests the Mongols over-ran China and established the Yuan Dynasty. This in turn was overthrown by the Ming Dynasty of native Chinese, but it wasn't until as late as 1400 that the Mongols ceased to hold power.

In England the Hundred Years War (1337–1453) was a period of conflict between England and France with perhaps eight major phases rather than continuous warfare. The war, which briefly featured Joan of Arc, ended with the fall of Bordeaux in 1453, leaving only Calais out of all the former extensive English possessions in France still in English hands. The three most famous battles – Agincourt, Crecy and Poitiers – all took place during the Hundred Years War.

The period also saw the Scottish wars with Edward I of England taking on Robert Bruce and William Wallace of Scotland. England had internal troubles too with Simon de Montfort's rebellion in 1263–5 and the Peasants' Revolt led by Wat Tyler in 1381.

The Wars of the Roses between the Houses of Lancaster and York lasted from 1455 to 1485 and caused some particularly bloody battles, even by Medieval standards.

On the continent of Europe, France, Germany and Italy all had internal struggles whilst in Spain the Moslems were continually being pushed back by Christian forces. The Swiss infantry came to the forefront as superb fighters and earned a reputation as hardy soldiers, much sought after as mercenaries.

The Crusades continued with five being conducted between 1202 and 1270. However, by 1291 the Moslems had retaken all the lands lost to the Crusaders.

The fall of Constantinople in 1204 marked the end of the Byzantine Empire, and while it continued for a further time, it was only a shadow of its former might.

In the middle of the 13th century the Seljuk Turks were overwhelmed by the Mongols but a new race, the Ottomans, established themselves in Eastern Europe.

Prevented from expanding westwards by Constantinople, the Ottomans themselves were defeated by the Tartars under their leader Tamerlane (1336–1405). Indeed Tamerlane also went on to wrest Egypt and Syria from the Mamelukes to found another empire in the Middle East.

Affairs in Eastern Europe were for a time dominated by John Ziska, who in the Hussite Wars in Bohemia (1419–1436), emerged as a military genius. One of his innovations was a field fortress constructed by the chaining together of wagons.

Major battles of the period include Agincourt (1415), Bannockburn (1314), Barnet (1471), Bosworth (1485), Crecy (1346), Evesham (1265), Falkirk (1298), Halidon Hill (1333), Morgarten

(1315), Northampton (1460), Poitiers (1356), Prague (1419), Sempach (1386), Sluys (1340), Tannenberg (1410), Tewkesbury (1471), Towton (1461) and Wakefield (1460).

Simple Wargame Rules for the Medieval Period

Movement: Knight full armoured and mounted 7"
Man-at-Arms mounted, but with lighter
  or less armour 9"
Light Cavalryman 12"
Knight or Man-at-Arms on foot 4"
Lesser armoured infantryman, crossbowman 6"
Archer 9"   [Units may move and fire]

Firing: Spear 6"   One dice per 10 figures able to
            Sling 12"   fire, apart from longbows who fire
            Bow 18"   one dice per 5 figures.
            Longbow 24"   Crossbowman may not move
            Crossbow 20"   and fire.

Score on the dice is the number of casualties inflicted, subject to the following cumulative amendments:
Moving and firing −1
Firing at over half range −1
Firing at fully armoured knights −2
Firing at armoured or shielded troops −1

Melee: The best method here is single combat, one dice per figure, highest wins, subject to the following:
Knight mounted and armoured first charging into melee, +3 to his dice.
Knight on subsequent melee moves still mounted, +2 to his dice.
Knight on foot, +1 to his dice.
Fighting troops that have shield or light armour, −1 to attacker's dice.
Completely unarmoured troops, −1 on dice or dice thrown for them.

At the end of melee count up casualties. The side with most – all units involved go back one move at the maximum speed for their type and spend the next move rallying. The winning side spends the next move after the melee rallying on the site of the melee and can then act as their general wishes. If the first round of the melee ends in a draw a second round is fought during the next game move. Melees can only last for two consecutive moves after which, if there is no outcome, both sides move back a full move and spend the subsequent one rallying. Both sides are then capable of action once more.

Suggested reading
Heath I., *Armies of the Middle Ages, Volume 1 (The Hundred Years War, The Wars of the Roses and the Burgundian Wars 1300–1487)* (WRG, 1982)

Heath I., *Armies of the Middle Ages, Volume 2 (The Ottoman Empire, Eastern Europe and the Near East 1300–1500)* (WRG, 1984)

Rothero C., *The Armies of Agincourt* (Osprey, 1981)

Rothero C., *The Armies of Crecy & Poitiers* (Osprey, 1981)

Rothero C., *The Scottish and Welsh Wars 1250–1400* (Osprey, 1984)

Wise T., *Medieval Heraldry* (Osprey, 1980)

Wise T., *Medieval Warfare* (Osprey, 1976)

Wise T., *The Wars of the Roses* (Osprey, 1983)

The Renaissance Period 1480–1697
This period of some two hundred years saw a great deal of military activity. The era of the mounted knight ended and infantrymen became the dominant force on the battlefield. The bow and crossbow gave way to the arquebusier and then the musket which improved rapidly in reliability, range and accuracy. The pike became the all important infantry equipment but this weapon itself fell into disuse by the end of the period.

17th century infantrymen in 15mm, suitable for several actions such as the Thirty Years War and the English Civil War.

Armour was rendered useless by the arrival of artillery and fell into virtually total disuse. Indeed the castle, hallmark of the earlier periods, was now badly compromised by increasing amounts of gunpowder and siege trains available to attackers. Gunpowder also brought about the limited use of hand grenades, primitive in nature and design, by the end of the period.

The English Civil Wars, of which there were three, spanned the period 1642–1651, and saw the execution of King Charles I and Oliver Cromwell installed as Lord Protector. With the restoration of the monarchy in 1660 the internal strife was subdued but English troops fought in various continental armies and wars. The Duke of Monmouth led a rebellion against James II and was defeated at Sedgemoor in 1685.

Prince Maurice of Nassau was commander of all the Dutch armies from 1590–1610 and in that period inflicted many defeats on the Spanish in the Netherlands and elsewhere.

A series of conflicts – The Italian Wars (1508–1514), the Valois-Hapsburg Wars (1515–1559) and the Wars of Religion (1560–1598) – saw the French continually at war with Spain and Italy in an attempt to become the chief power in Europe.

The Holy Roman Empire had many internal problems and was faced with opposition from Francis I of France and Charles V of Germany which kept Europe in a constant state of war in the first half of the 16th century.

The feared Swiss infantry began to lose their battlefield dominance due to the arrival of artillery and the increasing infantry firepower offered by the growing sophistication of gunpowder.

The Thirty Years' War (1618–1648) may have started as a war of religion between the Roman Catholics and Protestants in Germany, but it very soon became a political struggle between the Bourbons and the Hapsburgs.

The Nine Years' War, also termed the War of the Palatinate, the War of the Grand Alliance or the War of the League of Augsburg (1688–1697) was an anti-French affair, fought mainly in the Netherlands and provoked by Louis XIV of France, as indeed were the earlier Dutch Wars of 1652–1678.

Further afield, Charles X of Sweden declare war on Poland in the First Northern War 1665–1660 and Denmark clashed with Sweden in the Scanian War of 1675–1679. Russia and Poland were at odds between 1632 and 1666 and the Ottoman Empire was at its peak under Suleiman the Magnificent during the first quarter of the 16th century. Towards the end of the Renaissance

period the Empire was in decline, but was still very powerful.

In South America, the Aztecs were at the height of their power during the 1500–1518 period and the Inca empire in Peru flourished at the same time.

Spanish and Portuguese expeditions made inroads into these empires and brought back immense wealth for their mother countries.

Major battles of the 1480–1697 period include: Battle of the Dunes (1658), Breitenfeld (1631), Dreux (1562), Fleurus (1690), Flodden (1513), Lutzen (1632), Marignano (1515), Marston Moor (1644), Mohacs (1526), Naseby (1645), Neerwinden (1693), Nieuport (1600), Pavia (1525), Pinkie (1547), Ravenna (1512) and Steenkerke (1692).

Simple Wargame Rules for the Renaissance Period

Movement: Heavy Cavalry 9"
              Medium Cavalry 10"
              Light Cavalry 12"
              Infantry pikeman 6"
              Infantry musketeers 9"
                (or Arquebusiers etc.)
              Other Infantry 9"
              Light Horse Drawn Artillery 9"
              Heavy Artillery 4"

Firing: Cavalry pistol 4"   [One dice per 8 figures
              Bow 18"   able to fire]
              Arquebusier 10"
              Musket 12"

Wargame artillery in 25mm from the English Civil War period.

Light Artillery 24"
Heavy Artillery 36"
N.B. Arquebusiers and musketeers cannot move and fire in the same turn.
Infantry fire: Score on dice is the number of casualties inflicted, halved at over half range.
Cavalry fire: One dice per cavalryman, '6' on an ordinary dice to kill one figure.
Artillery fire: One dice per field gun, dice score is casualties, halved at over half range.

Melee: Points per figure are allotted to the various types of troops, one dice being thrown for every 10 points. The dice score gives the casualties inflicted on the enemy, also in points.
Pikemen 2
Musketeers/Arquebusiers 1½
Any other Foot Figures 1
Heavy Cavalry 3
Medium Cavalry 2
Light Cavalry 1

Normally the first two ranks of a unit are reckonable for melee purposes, but pike formations may count three ranks in a melee, whilst cavalry units may only count one. At the end of the melee count up the casualty points and remove the appropriate number of figures in a ratio proper to the mix of figure types involved in the melee. Any outstanding points can either be ignored or carried forward on a cumulative basis to the next melee.

The side which has lost the most points in the melee – not necessarily the most figures – must retreat one move and spend the next move rallying. The winning side rallies on the site of the melee for one move and is then capable of action once again on the following move.

If the melee is drawn after the first round, then a second round takes place in the next game move. If after this the melee outcome is still undecided, both sides retire one move and spend the next move rallying.

Suggested Reading
Asquith S., *The New Model Army 1645–60* (Osprey, 1981)
Gush G., *Renaissance Armies 1480–1650* (PSL, 1975)
Haythornthwaite P., *The English Civil War* (Blandford, 1983)
Rogers H., *Battles & Generals of the Civil Wars* (Seeley Service, 1968)
Wise T., *The Conquistadores* (Osprey, 1980)
Young P., *The English Civil War Armies* (Osprey, 1973)
Young P. & Holmes R., *The English Civil War* (Eyre Methuen, 1974)

The Marlburian Period 1700–1715
This period is dominated by John Churchill, 1st Duke of Marlborough, from whom it takes its name. His four famous actions against the French and their Bavarian allies at Blenheim, Ramillies, Oudenarde and Malplaquet are well-recorded. Generally in

Something of an Oriental flavour, two Gallia Japanese houses, ideal for Samurai wargames.

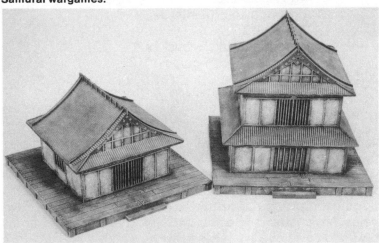

this period, however, commanders sought to avoid battles which would be costly to their small, highly professional armies and sieges became the predominant military activity.

The arrival of the bayonet saw the rapid decline of the pikeman, for now each musketeer could defend himself as well as firing at the enemy. Muskets, too, continued to improve and by the end of the period most armies were equipped with the flintlock variety. Hand grenades fell into disuse in the field and were retained only for use in sieges or assaults on defences.

The Great Northern War (1700–1721) saw Charles XII of Sweden taking on and defeating Peter the Great of Russia as well as the forces of Denmark, Norway, Poland-Saxony and Prussia. In a series of brilliant campaigns the Swedish commander won a string of victories only to be defeated at Poltava in 1709 by Peter the Great. Peter himself went on to invade Moldavia, Poland and Turkey as the fighting continued.

The War of the Spanish Succession 1701–1714 was brought about by the fact that Charles II of Spain had no direct heir, so Louis XIV of France nominated his grandson Philip of Anjou whilst Leopold I, the Hapsburg Emperor, nominated his son Archduke Charles.

England and Holland had no wish to see Spain united with either Austria or France and so stepped in.

Prince Eugene of Savoy clashed with the French in Italy and inflicted several defeats on them before the focus shifted to the Duke of Marlborough. Assisted by Eugene, the Duke won a

15mm Marlburian dragoons made by Peter Laing. Note that there are three figures to each base.

string of victories against a variety of French commanders. Eugene himself finally swept the French out of Italy in 1706, but in 1711 Marlborough was recalled due to political pressures and his military career was over.

The war also extended to Spain but, lacking the Duke's guidance, the Allied forces did not perform well there and after capturing Madrid were beaten at the battle of Almanza in 1707.

In July 1704 Gibraltar was captured by a force of British marines who successfully resisted a subsequent Franco-Spanish siege.

The ill-fated Jacobite Rebellion in Scotland took place in 1715 as supporters of James Edward Stuart 'The Pretender' tried to restore his throne.

While Marlborough's career was over, Prince Eugene continued to be active. In 1716–18 Austria was at war with Turkey and the Prince inflicted numerous defeats on the Turks, beating them comprehensively in several engagements.

Major battles of the period: Blenheim (1704), Chiari (1701), Cremona (1702), Hummselsdorf (1702), Malplaquet (1709), Narva (1700), Oudenarde (1708), Preston (1715) and Ramillies (1706).

Simple Wargame Rules for the Marlburian Period

Movement: Infantry/Dismounted Dragoons 6" (move & fire 3")
Cavalry/Dragoons 10" (if firing, 4")
Light Artillery 6" (artillery may not move and fire)
Heavy Artillery 3"

Firing: Cavalry Pistol 4" (French units only)
Musket 12"   [One dice per 8 figures able to fire]
Light Artillery 18"
Heavy Artillery 36"
Infantry fire: Score on dice is the number of casualties inflicted, halved at over half range.
Cavalry fire: One dice per cavalryman (N.B. French units only, British cavalry did not fire), '6' on an ordinary dice to kill one figure.
Artillery fire: One dice per gun, dice score is casualties, halved at over half range.

Melee: Infantrymen are worth 1 point in melee, cavalrymen 2 points each. One dice is thrown for every 10 points worth, +1 added to the score if the unit is charging. The dice score gives the casualties inflicted on the enemy, also in points. The first two ranks of a unit are counted in a melee.

The side which has lost the most points in the melee withdraws for one move and spends the next move rallying, the winning side rallies on the site of the melee for one move and is then capable of action once again. Melees continue until the outcome is decided.

Suggested Reading
Barthorp M., *Marlborough's Army 1702–11* (Osprey, 1980)
Barthorp M., *The Jacobite Rebellions 1689–1745* (Osprey, 1982)
Chandler D., *Marlborough as Military Commander* (Batsford, 1973)
Francis D., *The First Peninsular War 1702–1713* (Ernest Benn, 1975)
Green D., *Blenheim* (Collins, 1974)
Kemp A., *Weapons & Equipment of the Marlborough Wars* (Blandford, 1980)
McKay D., *Prince Eugene of Savoy* (Thames & Hudson, 1977)

The Mid-18th Century (1720-1772)
The flintlock musket was now standard issue to infantrymen and the weapon continued to improve. A new development in the form of rifled barrels began to appear from the middle of the period onwards. Muskets with rifled barrels – 'rifles' – tended to be the weapon of a new troop type, the light infantryman or skirmisher. Recruited initially from woodsmen and hunters these troops operated in loose, open formations ahead of the main mass of troops.

The mounted arm now mainly consisted only of medium cavalry with irregular lighter units being employed as scouts and raiders. Field artillery was still cumbersome but was far more organised and drilled than had previously been the case.

Cannister – a number of metal balls packed into a suitable container – was now used as an anti-personnel short range artillery weapon with devastating effect.

The period is identified by the manoeuvring of rigid blocks of troops, usually more afraid of their sergeants than of the enemy, capable of extremely fast and accurate rates of fire. While sieges did still occur, field actions were the accepted way to settle differences of opinion.

If the earlier part of the 18th century was dominated by the

The linear tactics employed by 18th century armies are clearly shown in this 'general 18th century battle' wargame.

Duke of Marlborough then the years following were firmly controlled by Frederick the Great of Prussia. Frederick must be noted as one of the greatest generals of history and a master of tactics. His string of victories from 1740–1763 were nearly always achieved with inferior numbers but superior tactics.

The War of Austrian Succession (1740–48) saw Austria (the Holy Roman Empire), England, the Netherlands and Russia allied against Bavaria, France, Prussia, Spain and Sweden. The main protagonists, however, were always Prussia under Frederick and Austria under Maria Theresa.

The war encompassed two small affairs, the first Silesian War (1740–42) and the Second Silesian War (1744–45) in which Frederick seized Silesia, but became isolated from his allies. In 1743 King George II of England, and also elector of Hanover, collected a multinational army in Germany which went on to beat the French at Dettingen. As a point of interest, this was to be the last time that a British monarch personally commanded an army in the field.

The Seven Years' War (1756–63) was caused by Frederick seeking to strengthen his hold on the newly acquired Silesia. Ranked against him were Austria, France, Russia and Saxony, but Frederick had the support of England and Hanover. After a string of victories, Frederick emerged from the war as an eminent general and Prussia as a great military power.

The Seven Years' War spread beyond Europe with battles in India, notably Plassey 1757, and America with the French and Indian War. In fact anywhere where the colonial interests of England and France clashed, the war was used as a convenient excuse for active arguing.

In 1745 Scottish Highlanders were involved with the Young Pretender, Prince Charles Edward (Bonny Prince Charlie), in the dual aims of independence from England and placing a Stuart on the throne. After a series of battles, the Highlanders were severely mauled at the battle of Culloden in 1746 and the attempt came to an end.

The Polish nation had more than its share of fighting during this period with the War for the Polish Throne (1733–68) and then the country's struggle for national independence (1768–72). In the latter war Russia sent troops into Poland, a move unsuccessfully resisted by the Poles. Prussia and Austria joined Poland to prevent the country being totally dominated by Russia, but an unhappy partition resulted.

Major battles: Culloden (1746), Dettingen (1743), Fontenoy (1745), Hohenfriedburg (1745), Kunersdorff (1759), Leuthen (1757), Lobositz (1756), Minden (1759), Mollwitz (1741), Plassey (1757) and Quebec (1759).

Simple Wargame Rules for the Mid-18th Century
Movement: Line Infantry 6" (move & fire 3")
            Light Infantry 8" (move & fire 6")

A superb example of scratch-built fortifications, in this case a recreation of the style dominant in the 18th century.

15mm Indians from Frei Korps 15, suitable for the Seven Years War in North America. (Photo Frei Korps 15)

Firing:

Other Infantry 9" (Highlanders, Indians etc.)
Light Cavalry 12"
Medium Cavalry 10"
Heavy Cavalry 9"
Light Artillery 8"
Medium Artillery 6"
Heavy Artillery 3"
Cavalry Pistol 4"   [One dice per 8 figures
Cavalry Carbine 8"   able to fire]
Musket 12"
Spears, Tomahawks etc. 3"
Light Artillery 18"
Medium Artillery 24"
Heavy Artillery 3 36"

Infantry fire: Score on dice is the number of casualties inflicted, halved at over half range.

Cavalry fire: One dice per cavalryman – '6' on an ordinary dice to kill one figure.

Artillery fire: One dice per gun, dice score are casualties halved at over half range, +1 if under 9" (cannister range).

Melee:

Infantry are worth 1 point in melee, light cavalry 2, medium cavalry 3 and heavy cavalry 4 points each. One dice is thrown for every 20 points worth, +1 added to the score if the unit is charging.

The dice score gives the casualties inflicted on the enemy, also in points.

The first two ranks of a unit are counted in a melee. The side which has lost the most points in the melee withdraws for one move and spends the next move rallying. The winning side rallies on the site of the melee for one move and is then capable of action once again. Melees will continue until the outcome has been decided.

A selection of settlers, rangers and infantrymen from the French and Indian war range available from Frei Korps 15. (Photo Frei Korps 15)

Suggested Reading

Barthorp M., *The Jacobite Rebellions 1689–1745* (Osprey, 1982)

Bence-Jones M., *Clive of India* (Constable, 1974)

Duffy C., *The Army of Frederick the Great* (David & Charles, 1974)

Duffy C., *The Army of Maria Theresa* (David & Charles, 1977)

Funcken L&F., *Arms & Uniforms: The Lace Wars* (Ward Lock, 1977)

May R., *Wolfe's Army* (Osprey, 1974)

Mollo J., *Uniforms of the Seven Years War 1756–63 (Blandford, 1977)*

Rogers H., *The British Army of the Eighteenth Century* (George Allen & Unwin, 1977)

Seaton A., *The Austro-Hungarian Army of the Seven Years War* (Osprey, 1973)

Seaton A., *Frederick the Great's Army* (Osprey, 1973)

Stacey C., *Quebec 1759* (Pan, 1973)

Tomasson K. & Buist F., *Battles of the '45* (Pan, 1967)

Windrow M., *Montcalm's Army* (Osprey, 1973)

The American War of Independence (1775-1783)

Long-standing differences between the thirteen American colonies and Great Britain broke into open rebellion when, in April 1775, a force of British soldiers moved to seize colonists' weapons held at Concord. The British troops met colonists at Lexington and shots were exchanged and thus started the War of Independence in which the American colonists wrested themselves from British control.

In June 1775 the Battle of Bunker Hill, or more accurately Breed's Hill, while technically a British victory gave the Colonial militiamen's cause a tremendous lift. The following month George Washington assumed command of all American continental forces to put the colonists on a proper military footing. It should not, however, be assumed that all the colonists were opposed to

British rule. Some colonists, termed 'tories', favoured it and fought hard alongside the British troops.

In 1776/7 in a British thrust against the New York area, the Battles of Harlem Heights (16 Sept), White Plains (28 Oct), Trenton (26 Dec) and Princeton (3 Jan) took place. Trenton is particularly interesting, for here some of the German mercenary troops employed by the British government were badly mauled by Washington's men. Colloquially referred to as Hessians, the capable mercenaries in fact came from the minor German states of Anspach-Bayreuth, Anhalt-Zerbst, Brunswick-Luneberg, Hesse-Hanau and Waldeck.

Hesse-Cassel provided more troops than all the other states put together, but the overall total of mercenary troops in the war was around 30,000 men.

The Germans fought in virtually every campaign of the war, and were only absent in the southern actions.

During 1777 the British commanders planned a three-pronged attack designed to split the colonies apart. The culmination of the campaign were the actions at Freemans Farm in September and Bemis Heights the following month, referred to as the battles of Saratoga. The British general Burgoyne lost them both and surrendered.

The other major battle of the year was in October at German-town where the British under General Howe defeated a numeric-ally superior force of Americans under George Washington. In February the following year, 1778, a Franco-American alliance was signed and French troops added their numbers to Washington's forces. June of the same year saw the drawn battle of Monmouth fought between Washington and Sir Henry Clinton.

In the southern part of the colonies, notably North and South Carolina, the war had been largely a guerrilla affair, with small raids and actions by both sides.

It was not until 1780 that the larger battles of Camden (16 Aug) and King's Mountain (7 Oct) took place. King's Mountain is particularly noteworthy since the troops on both sides in the action were all Americans.

The following year, 1781, saw Cowpens (17 Jan), Guilford Courthouse (15 March) and Eutaw Springs (8 Sept). Cowpens was an American victory but the others and several minor actions were all British successes. In spite of this, however, British troops had to withdraw and by the end of 1781 had left the area completely.

The final campaign of the War ended with the Siege of Yorktown in September and October 1781. On 19 October of that year General Cornwallis, the commander of the British forces in Yorktown, surrendered to Washington and his French allies. To all intents and purposes the war was over and the Americans had won.

Simple Wargame Rules for the American War of Independence

Movement: Line Infantry 6"
Light Infantry 9"
Militiamen 5"
Cavalry 12"
Artillery 6"

Firing: Musket 12" (one dice per 8 figures)
Rifle 18" (one dice per figure)
Artillery 24"
Musket fire: Score on dice is the number of casualties inflicted, halved at over half range.
Rifle fire: One dice per figure so armed. '5' or '6' to kill one figure, '6' only if over half range.
Artillery fire: One dice per gun, dice score is casualties, halved at over half range, +1 if under 9" (cannister range).

Melee: Infantry are worth 1 point in melee, cavalry 2 points. One dice is thrown for every 10 points +1 added to score if unit concerned is charging, –1 if it is a unit of militiamen.
The dice score gives the casualties inflicted on the enemy, also in points.
The first two ranks of a unit are countable in a melee.

The side which has lost the most points in the melee withdraws for one move and spends the next move rallying. The winning side rallies on the site of the melee for one move and is then capable of action again. Melees continue until the outcome has been decided.

Suggested Reading

Johnson C., *Battles of the American Revolution* (Sampson Low, 1975)
Katcher P., *The American Provincial Corps 1775–1784* (Osprey, 1973)
Kemp A., *American Soldiers of the Revolution* (Almark, 1972)

Kemp A., *The British Army in the American Revolution* (Almark, 1973)

May R., *The British Army in North America 1775–1783* (Osprey, 1974)

Mollo J., *Uniforms of the American Revolution* (Blandford, 1975)

Young P., *George Washington's Army* (Osprey, 1972)

The Napoleonic Period 1792–1815

This is one of the most popular wargame periods. Dominated by the man from which it takes its name, these twenty odd years saw France rise from the confusion of the Revolution, go on to be Europe's strongest nation and then fall into disarray.

Napoleon Bonaparte (1769–1821) rose to be First Consul of France in November 1799 and the country's Emperor in December 1804. One of history's greatest generals, Napoleon won many victories, but in the final analysis he ran out of men, time and luck as his enemies proportionally increased and then concentrated their forces.

The period can be split into nine main phases and these, along with their major battles, are listed below.

War of the First Coalition 1792–98
Jemappes (1792), Neerwinden (1792), Valmy (1792).

War of the Second Coalition 1798–1800
Genoa (1799), Hohenlinden (1800), Marengo (1800).

The Egyptian Campaign 1798–1800
Aboukir (1799), Mount Tabor (1799), The Pyramids (1798).

The War of the Third Coalition 1805–1807
Auerstadt (1806), Austerlitz (1805), Eylau (1807), Friedland (1807), Jena (1806).

The Peninsular War 1806–1814
Bussaco (1810), Corunna (1809), Fuentes d'Onoro (1811), Orthez (1814), Salamanca (1812), Sorauren (1813), Talavera (1809), Toulouse (1814), Vimeiro (1808), Vittorio (1813).

The War with Russia 1812
Borodino (1812), Crossing the Berezina (1812), Krasnoi (1812), Smolensk (1812), Valutino (1812).

The Leipzig Campaign 1813
Bautzen (1813), Dresden (1813), Kulm (1813), Leipzig (1813), Lutzen (1813).

The Defence of France 1814
Many small, well fought but desperate actions, for example Arcis-Sur-Aube, Craonne, La Fere Champenoise, Laon, Monte-

French Napoleonic light cavalry in 25mm: Chasseurs à Cheval of Napoleon's Imperial Guard.

reau and Rheims.

In April 1814 Napoleon abdicated to exile on the island of Elba.

The Hundred Days 1815

Ligny (1815), Quatre Bras (1815), Waterloo (1815), Wavre (1815).

In June 1815 Napoleon abdicated for the second time. On this occasion he was sent to St Helena where he died in 1821.

Another leading figure of the period was the Duke of Wellington who consistently beat Napoleon's marshals in the Peninsular war and the great man himself at Waterloo. The Duke probably vies with Marlborough for the accolade of the supreme English commander of all time.

The Napoleonic Wars have an almost magnetic attraction for wargamers, with Waterloo surely ranking as the most popular battle, both for study and re-fighting as a wargame.

The campaigns and battles are well documented, as are the lives of the personalities involved. Few eras of history can produce such glamorous figures as Napoleon's Marshals or such able commanders as Sir John Moore, the Prussian Blucher and the Archduke Charles of Austria.

One other war frequently overlooked is the 1812–15 war between the United States and England. Due to a dispute over naval rights, the war finally decided little but kept the Americans

Wargames scenery: On view are wall sections, a bridge and lengths of river all made from vac-formed plastic.

out of British Canada and the British Navy away from American vessels.

Simple Wargame Rules for the Napoleonic Period

Movement: Infantry 6"
Light Infantry 9"
Light Cavalry 15"
Medium Cavalry 12"
Heavy Cavalry 9"
Medium Artillery 6"
Heavy Artillery 3"

Firing: Musket 12" (one dice per 8 figures)
Rifle 18"
Carbine 6"
Medium Artillery 24"
Heavy Artillery 36"

Musket fire: Score on the dice is the number of casualties inflicted, halved at over half range.

Carbine & Rifle fire (and Muskets if desired): One dice per figure so armed. '5' or '6' to kill one figure, '6' only if over half range.

Artillery fire: One dice per gun, dice score are casualties, halved at over half range, +1 under 9" (cannister range).

Melee: Infantry and light infantry are worth 1 point in a melee, light cavalry 2 points, medium cavalry 3 points and heavy cavalry 4 points. One dice is thrown for every 20 points, +1 added if unit is charging.

The dice score gives the casualties inflicted on the enemy, also in points. The first two ranks are countable in a melee.

The side which has lost the most points in the melee withdraws for one move and spends the next move rallying. The winning side rallies on the site of the melee for one move and is then capable of action again. Melees will continue until the outcome has been decided.

Suggested Reading

Barthorpe M., *Wellington's Generals* (Osprey, 1978)

Cassin-Scott J., *Uniforms of the Napoleonic Wars in Colour* (Blandford, 1973)

Chandler D., *Dictionary of the Napoleonic Wars* (MacMillan, 1979)

Fosten B., *Wellington's Infantry* (Osprey, 1981)

Fosten B., *Wellington's Light Cavalry* (Osprey, 1982)

Fosten B., *Wellington's Heavy Cavalry* (Osprey, 1982)

Funcken L&F., *Arms & Uniforms: The Napoleonic Wars* (2 parts) (Ward Lock, 1973)

Haythornthwaite P., *Uniforms of the French Revolutionary Wars* (Blandford, 1981)

Haythornthwaite P., *Uniforms of Waterloo in Colour* (Blandford, 1974)

Haythornthwaite P., *Napoleon's Line Infantry* (Osprey, 1983)

Lachouque H., *Napoleon's War in Spain* (A & AP, 1982)

Lachouque H., *Waterloo* (A & AP, 1972)

Lawford J., *Napoleon's Last Campaigns 1813–15* (Sampson Low, 1977)

Von Pivka O., *Armies of the Napoleonic Era* (David & Charles, 1979)

Von Pivka O., *Dutch Belgian Troops of the Napoleonic Wars* (Osprey, 1980)

Windrow M., *Military Dress of the Peninsular War* (Ian Allen, 1974)

Wise T., *Artillery Equipments of the Napoleonic Wars* (Osprey, 1979)

Wise T., *Flags of the Napoleonic Wars: Volume 1* (Osprey, 1978)
Wise T., *Flags of the Napoleonic Wars: Volume 2* (Osprey, 1978)
Wise T., *Flags of the Napoleonic Wars: Volume 3* (Osprey, 1981)

Wars of the Later 19th Century

The latter half of the 19th century saw many changes in weaponry and hence in tactics. Artillery changed from the well established smooth-bore muzzle-loading variety to the rifled breech-loading system. The then familiar round, solid cannon-balls were phased out, to be replaced by shells fitted with fuses.

Rudimentary, but ever more sophisticated, machine guns of various types made their appearance and were firmly established in army arsenals by the end of the century. Muskets had been replaced by single-shot muzzle-loading rifles and these in turn gave way to repeating rifles with rapid fire made possible by the addition of magazines of ammunition. Ranges, too, increased until rifle fire could outrange the murderous short range artillery cannister fire.

All these weapon improvements radically affected tactics on the battlefield. Napoleonic-like masses of the Crimean War had no place in the wars later in the century. Indeed the American

A superb Afghan fort built by Ian Weekley of 'Battlements'. Such a piece can form a fitting centre for a wargame scenario. (Photo I. Weekley)

Civil War saw the beginnings of trench warfare as the battlefield soldier was forced to seek whatever cover he could in the face of ever-increasing firepower.

As with the Napoleonic period, the 19th century has been divided here into its major wars or campaigns, with the major battles listed.

The Crimean War 1853–56
The Alma (1854), Siege of Sevastopol (Oct 1854–Sept 1855), Balaklava (1854) and Inkerman (1854).
War of Austria with France & Piedmont 1859
Magenta and Solferino
Austro-Prussian (Seven Weeks) War 1866
Koniggratz (or Sadowa)
Franco-Prussian War 1870–71
This period has recently come into favour with wargamers, with numerous new ranges of well-sculpted figures available. It is to be hoped that the wargame re-creation is more enjoyable than the actual event. Bismarck gathered Germany under his Prussian banner into an anti-French league. This was unexpected by the French under their Emperor Napoleon III who decided to attack Prussia in order to strike the first blow. The French lost every

A wargame staged by the Victorian Military Society involving a river crossing on the North-West Frontier of India, late in the 19th century. The figures in use are 30mm Tradition. (Photo R. Bendall)

major action and suffered humiliating defeat. Major actions in 1870 were Gravelotte – St. Privat, Mars – La-Tour, Rezonville, Sedan, Spicheren and Vionville.

The siege of Paris lasted from September 1870 to January 1871, when the city capitulated.

Unification of Italy 1850–1870

Northern Italy was occupied by the Austro-Hungarian empire who dominated all of Italy. Based on Piedmont (Sardinia), Giuseppe Garibaldi launched a successful campaign which united Italy and threw off the Austrians' yoke.

Egypt and the Sudan 1882–98

A British army with Egyptian and Sudanese troops took on the Mahdi and his native followers who had declared Holy War.

Tel El-Kebir (1882), Siege of Khartoum (1884–5), Atbara (1898) and Omdurman (1898).

The Zulu War 1879

Another British 'small war' when the Zulu nation rose against British rule.

Isandhlwana, Kambla, Ulundi.

First Boer War 1880–81

The Boer settlers in South Africa came into conflict with Britain.

Laing's Nek (1881), Majuba Hill (1881). As an aside, it is generally thought that Laing's Nek was the last action in which the British Army actually carried colours into battle.

Second Boer War 1899–1902

Colenso (1899), Magersfontein (1899), Modder River (1899).

Second Afghan War 1880

This is another example of the numerous campaigns which involved the British army in the latter half of the 19th century. The British soldier fought all over the world.

Maiwand (July) and Kandahar (Sept).

US Indian Wars 1850–98

The US army campaigned against the American Indian tribes for a number of years. Large battles were rare and the wars consisted of Indian raids and attempted army reprisals.

Notable actions are the Fetterman Massacre (1866), The Little Big Horn (1876) and Wounded Knee (1890).

The American Civil War 1861–65

A firm wargames favourite in the early years of the hobby, the American Civil War has only recently begun to emerge from a prolonged period of apparent disfavour. The war is interesting from a number of standpoints; had the lessons its course threw up been digested then arguably the Franco-Prussian war and

Chinese Boxers assault the Legation Quarter of Peking during a Boxer Rebellion 1900 wargame using 25mm figures. (Photo I. Knight)

indeed the First World War could have followed different courses. Also, the ironclad warships of both sides, small and clumsy as they were, revolutionised naval ship building and rendered traditional wooden vessels obsolete.

To summarise a major conflict in a few paragraphs is impossible and only the major campaigns and battles can be mentioned here.

The eleven Southern or Confederate States of America seceded from their twenty-two Northern or Union neighbouring states, mainly to protect their agricultural system which was based on slave labour.

There were two theatres of war, East and West, and it is under those two headings that they will be considered.

The War in the East The first major action was First Bull Run in July 1861, when the Confederate General Jackson earned his nickname 'Stonewall' for his part in the victory. This was followed by more battles in May and June of the following year – Front Royal, First Winchester, Cross Keys and Port Republic. Then followed a series of actions called the Seven Days battles – Mechanicsville, Gaines's Mill and Malvern Hill among others – where the Confederates lost, but it was the Union troops who were pushed out of the area around Richmond, the southern capital during the war. There then followed three short campaigns – Second Bull Run (Manassas), Antietam (Sharpsburg) and Fredericksburg. May 1863 had the battle of Chancellorsville, a Confederate victory, which saw the death of the stalwart General Jackson. The next month saw the battle of Brandy Station, the largest cavalry action of the war and then in July came the war's largest battle, Gettysburg, which lasted three days and was a Union victory.

The war in the East finished with the battles of Spotsylvania and Yellow Tavern in May and Cold Harbor in June, followed by the Siege of Petersburg which lasted until 31 December 1864.

The War in the West Opening in August 1861 with a Confederate tactical victory at Wilson's Creek, the war in the West was fought both east and west of the Mississippi river and contained numerous relatively small actions.

April 1862 saw the Union victory at Shiloh, whilst the battle of Corinth (October) and Stones River (Murfreesboro) 31 December to 3 January 1863 were the next major actions.

The main event of 1863 was the Vicksburg campaign which saw the Union forces under General Grant begin to gain the upper hand and which culminated in the siege of the town from 19 May to 4 July when the garrison surrendered. The rest of the year was taken up with the Chattanooga, Chickamauga and Tullahoma campaigns which resulted in some fierce battles. In

A Federal camp under attack during an American Civil War wargame. The figures are 25mm and the tents are scratch-built from paper.

1864 the Union General Sherman advanced in devastating fashion into Confederate Georgia, its capital Atlanta falling at the end of August.

On 9 April 1865 the Confederate General Lee surrendered his army at Appomattax Courthouse and the war was over.

Other American Wars

In 1898 the Spanish-American War took place, involving an American expedition to Cuba. The following year, 1899, General MacArthur took an American force to the Philippines to deal with an insurrection there.

Britain, France and Spain in 1861 sent a joint expedition to Mexico, notable for the battle of Camerone in 1863 where 65 French Foreign Legionaries held off 2000 Mexicans.

The end of the 19th century saw many wars between the various Latin American countries as each struggled for independence and recognition.

The Boxer Rebellion 1900

As the century drew to a close an uprising of the Chinese Boxer Society required the combined attention of Austria, France, Germany, Great Britain, Italy, Japan, Russia and the United States before it was quelled.

This is a period rich in choice for the wargamer. Great Britain was busy creating and defending her large Empire, the Americans were in fierce battle and Europe was locked in conflict as the various Continental nations vied for prominence.

Simple Wargame Rules for the Later 19th Century

Movement: Infantry 6"

Natives on foot 9"

Native Cavalry 15"

Regular Cavalry 12"

Artillery (including MGs) 6"

Firing: Rifle 24"

Musket 12"

Carbine 8"

Gatling Gun (etc.) 20"

Artillery 48"

Rifle fire: One dice per 5 figures. Score on the dice is the number of casualties inflicted, −1 at over half range.

Carbine and Musket fire: One dice per 10 figures (usually only natives or irregulars still had muskets

A Wild West shoot-out using 54mm figures in an authentic setting.

in this period). Dice score are casualties, halved at over half range.

Machine Gun fire: Three dice per weapon – score counts as casualties – halved at over half range. One dice rolled every time the machine gun fires, a '1' and gun malfunctions and may not fire that turn, but OK for next.

Artillery fire: Two dice per gun, dice score are casualties, halved at over half range, +1 under 12".

Melees: A less frequent occurrence on European battlefields but still the case with disciplined troops versus natives. 1 point per foot figure, 2 for a cavalryman except for lancers which are 3 points on the first move of melee only, after that, 2 points.

One dice per 20 points – dice score gives casualties inflicted on the enemy, in points.

All figures in a unit are eligible for the melee and the melee will continue until outcome is decided.

Suggested Reading

Baring Pemberton W., *Battles of the Boer War* (Pan, 1969)
Baring Pemberton W., *Battles of the Crimean War* (Pan, 1968)
Bodin L., *The Boxer Rebellion* (Osprey, 1979)

Brown P., *Bury My Heart at Wounded Knee* (Barrie & Jenkins, 1970)

Chisholm R., *Ladysmith* (Osprey, 1979)

Commager H. (ed), *Illustrated History of the American Civil War* (Orbis, 1976)

Compton P., *The Last Days of General Gordon* (Robert Hale, 1974)

Dillon R., *North American Indian Wars* (A & AP, 1983)

Edwardes M., *A Season in Hell* (Hamish Hamilton, 1973)

Griffith K., *Thank God We Kept The Flag Flying* (Hutchinson, 1974)

Hibbert C., *The Great Mutiny* (Allen Lane, 1978)

Horns K., *The Fall of Paris 1870–71* (MacMillan, 1965)

Hunt C. & Embleton G., *The American Civil War* (Almark, 1974)

Llewellyn A., *The Siege of Delhi* (MacDonald & Janes, 1977)

May R. & Embleton G., *The Franco-Prussian War* (Almark, 1975)

Morris D., *The Washing of the Spears* (Sphere, 1968)

Robson B., *The Road to Kabul* (A & AP, 1986)

Woods F. (ed), *Young Winston's Wars* (Leo Cooper, 1972)

Ziegler P., *Omdurman* (Collins, 1973)

The First World War 1914–18

The First World War, or the Great War as it was called at the time, was to become the first 'total war'. The home front came into being and it was the agricultural and manufacturing capabilities of a country that became the predominant factors. Certainly there were still armies, now vast in size, deployed in the field, but it was the technical and logistical support of these troops that was to become of paramount importance.

The ever-increasing power of weapons stultified strategy and

A 15mm Wild West stage coach complete with horse team, driver, guard and passengers from Frei Korps 15. (Photo Frei Korps 15)

while the war opened and closed with manoeuvre, the large middle section was a war of stagnation.

The so-called 'Race to the Sea' saw the opponents on what was to be termed the Western Front trying to outflank one another. Eventually they ran out of land and only costly frontal attacks could resolve the stalemate.

Artillery became an increasingly important factor which, in combination with the rapidly increasing number of machine guns, plus barbed wire and trenches, deterred frontal assaults on positions.

The armoured tank emerged from the conflict as the major new weapon as the usefulness and value of horsed cavalry declined in the face of ever-increasing defensive firepower.

For the first time war acquired a third dimension with the aeroplane – initially intended as a reconnaissance replacement for the observation balloon – becoming a useful and deadly weapon.

To summarise meaningfully the events of four years is difficult. The main concentration here will be on the major battles of the Western Front, with limited coverage of the more important aspects of other theatres of the war.

In June 1914 the assassination in Sarajevo of Archduke Franz Ferdinand, heir to the Austro-Hungarian throne, pushed the Triple Alliance of Germany, Austria-Hungary and Italy into war with the Triple Entente of France, Great Britain and Russia.

The German forces moved in accordance with the heavily modified plan originally worked out by General von Schlieffen in the event of a two-front war against France and Russia. The movements of the French troops was in accordance with 'Plan XVII', with the British Expeditionary Force landing on the Continent in support.

The Western Front 1914 saw several major battles, Mons (23 Aug), Le Cateau (25 Aug–7 Sept), The Marne (5–10 Sept) and 1st Ypres (30 Oct–24 Nov). This last action saw the British Expeditionary Force suffering extremely heavy casualties.

The following year, 1915, witnessed the first use of poison gas in the West at 2nd Ypres (22 April–5 May). Other major actions included Vimy Ridge (16 May–30 June, 25 Sept–30 Oct) and Loos (25 Sept–14 Oct).

In May 1915 Italy, having left the Triple Alliance, declared war on Austria and there was heavy fighting in northern Italy in and around the Isonzo.

An assembled but as yet unpainted 1/76 white metal kit of a 1914 Rolls Royce armoured car by Scale Link.

The major events of 1916 were the battle of Verdun (21 Feb–18 Dec) and the 1st Battle of the Somme (24 June–13 Nov), both epic encounters in their own right.

In April 1917 the United States joined the war and the battle of Cambrai (20 Nov–3 Dec) saw tanks used in significant numbers of the first time. Other major actions included Arras (9–15 April), Messines (7 June), Passchendaele (31 July–10 Nov) and Caporetto (24 Oct–12 Nov). This last battle took place in Northern Italy and was also called the 12th Battle of Isonzo.

Paris suffered an artillery bombardment from March to August 1918 and the early part of the year saw three major German offensives. These were halted and the second half of the year saw Allied counter-offensives which ended with the Armistice in November.

Major actions: Chateau-Thierry, Belleau Wood (30 May–17 June) and 2nd Battle of the Marne (15–17 July).

The Eastern Front and other Theatres In August 1914 Russia invaded East Prussia in what was to become the Tannenburg campaign. August saw the battle of Tannenburg and September the 1st Battle of the Masurian Lakes.

Austria invaded Serbia, fighting developed in Poland and in October, Turkey declared war on the members of the Triple Entente.

1915 saw fighting in the Balkans, the 2nd Battle of the

Masurian Lakes in February and the badly-mounted Gallipoli landings took place in April and August.

During 1916 there was fighting in Arabia, Egypt, Mesopotamia and Palestine which continued into 1917 with several battles at Gaza. The Russian revolution of 1917 plunged that country in chaos and effectively took her out of the war.

The final year of the war saw major actions in Italy – The Piave (15 June), Monte Grappo (23 Oct) and Vittorio Veneto (25 Oct–4 Nov) – as well as fighting in the Caucasus, Palestine and Syria.

Mention should also be made of two other figures who were active during the war. In East Africa the German Von Lettow-Vurbeck carried out a guerrilla campaign against the British forces there for four years and was never caught, and T.E. Lawrence (Lawrence of Arabia) led an Arab rebellion against the Turks and managed to keep over 25,000 of their troops tied down as a result.

Simple Wargame Rules for World War I

Movement: Infantry 6"
Cavalry 8"
Tanks 6"
Armoured cars, lorries, etc. 10"
Field Artillery 6"

Firing: Rifle 24"
Machine gun 24"
Tank gun 48"
Field gun 60"

Rifle fire: One dice per figure, '5' or '6' kills, '4-6' under half range.

Machine gun: Three dice per weapon, score counting as casualties, halved at over half range.

Tank & Field guns: Two dice per gun, dice score are casualties, halved at over half range, +1 under 20".

Field gun or Tank firing on Tank: Two dice per gun, 11 or 12 scored, tank knocked out, 9-10 tank disabled for one turn, may not move or fire. Less than 9, no effect. Halving or +1 does not apply in this case.

Field gun or Tank firing on Armoured car, lorry etc: Two dice per gun, 10-12 scored, target knocked out, 8-9, disabled for one turn, may not move or fire. Less than 8 no effect. Halving or +1 does not apply in this case.

Melees: Not really applicable to this period, but if necessary, one dice per figure eligible, highest score wins.

Suggested Reading
Ascoli D., *The Mons Star* (Harrap, 1981)
Blond G., *Verdun* (White Lion Publishing, 1976)
Carew T., *Wipers: The First Battle of Ypres* (Hamish Hamilton, 1974)
Cooper B., *Tank Battles of World War I* (Ian Allan, 1974)
Farrar-Hockley A., *The Somme* (Pan, 1983)
Liddel-Hart B., *History of the First World War* (Cassell, 1970)
Masters J., *Fourteen Eighteen* (Michael Joseph, 1965)
Mollo A., *Army Uniforms of World War I* (Blandford, 1977)
Nash D., *Imperial German Army Handbook 1914–1918* (Ian Allan, 1980)
Stokesbury J., *A Short History of World War I* (Robert Hale, 1982)
Terraine J., *The Western Front 1914–1918* (Hutchinson, 1964)
Warner P., *The Battle of Loos* (William Kimber, 1976)

The Second World War 1939-45
Preceded by the Spanish Civil War (1936–1939), the Second World War became a conflict of global proportions. On the one side, the Axis powers, Germany and Italy, were supported by Japan and some Eastern European countries, while arrayed against them were the British Commonwealth, Belgium, Denmark, France, Greece, Holland, Norway, Poland, the United States and Yugoslavia.

While it is true to say that the main theatre of war was in Europe, several other important actions took place, notably in North Africa and the islands in the Pacific Ocean.

1939
The war opened with the German attack on Poland in September.

German soldiers of the Third Reich – WW2 Waffen SS, from Platoon 20. (Photo Model Figures & Hobbies)

The British and French armies mobilised but remained behind the Maginot Line, a period which has been termed 'the phoney war' due to the lack of military action.

Russia began to organise her Baltic neighbours, a move rejected by Finland. The resulting Finnish-Russian war lasted from November 1939 to March 1940 when Finland, after a gallant struggle, capitulated.

1940

The Germans efficiently conquered Denmark and Norway and invaded the Low Countries.

In May both Belgium and Holland fell and later that month some 338,000 Allied soldiers were evacuated from Dunkirk in Northern France. This in turn led to the Allied evacuation of Norway and the capitulation of France.

The German leader Adolf Hitler, against the advice of many of his generals, decided to invade England. Since the German navy could not match the Royal Navy, the German Luftwaffe was tasked with firstly defeating the Royal Air Force and then disabling the Royal Navy. Thus began the Battle of Britain which lasted from August to October, with the German plans finally being cancelled as a result of the defence put up by the Royal Air Force and the Royal Navy.

In the Western Desert in North Africa General Wavell threw the Italians out of Egypt, while back in Europe, Italian troops invaded Greece and Southern France.

1941

Wavell's offensives continued, but General Rommel appeared on the scene, in command of the German Afrika Korps, and immediately launched successful counter-attacks. The Allied forces, now consisting of the newly named Eighth Army, fought a series of actions with the Afrika Korps, cancelling most of Rommel's gains as the year progressed.

**Something unusual, a group of WW2 Partisans from Platoon 20.
Note figure fourth from left throwing a Molotov cocktail.
(Photo Model Figures & Hobbies)**

April saw the conquest of Greece by the Germans and May saw the first major airborne assault in history as the island of Crete also fell into German hands.

Two more significant events took place during 1941, the German invasion of Russia and the Japanese attack on the US naval base at Pearl Harbor, which brought the Americans into the war.

1942

Britain mounted two raids against enemy-occupied France at St. Nazaire, which was a success, and at Dieppe, which was a total failure.

The main theatre of war continued to be the Western Desert with the Eighth Army now led by General Montgomery in action at Alam Halfa (31 Aug–7 Sept) and at El Alamein (23 Oct–Nov).

A joint British and American venture, 'Operation Torch', successfully seized Algeria, Morocco and Tunisia as Allied bases in North Africa.

In Russia the war was one of offensive and counter-offensive as first the Russians and then the Germans attacked. The battle for Stalingrad lasted from August to December and ultimately saw the collapse of the German front.

1943

The Axis hold in North Africa was ended in May as Rommel's troops were beaten in a number of battles, but only after a long struggle.

In July the British Eighth Army and American 7th Army invaded Sicily, moving on to invade Southern Italy three months later.

In February the German forces at Stalingrad surrendered and Soviet offensives recaptured all the land lost during the previous year. The Germans recaptured the town of Kharkov and in July the battle of Kursk – a major tank action – took place.

1944

The Allied advance northwards through Italy continued, supported by landings at Anzio early in the year. On 4 June Allied units entered Rome and advanced on the Gothic line in Northern Italy.

By far the biggest event of the year, or of the war for that matter, was Operation Overlord, the Allied invasion of France, which took place in June and July. Preceded by airborne troops, the greatest amphibious assault ever mounted was delivered against the Normandy coast. Beach-heads were speedily established and troops pushed inland. Paris was liberated in August and by September the Allies were close to the German border.

In August American and French troops landed in southern France to add their weight to the attack.

In September airborne units were sent in ahead of the main Allied forces to open a route for a speedy advance straight into Germany. The battle of Arnhem (17–26 Sept) resulted and the ambitious plan was foiled by the Germans.

A German counter-offensive in the Ardennes region very late in the year resulted in the battle for Bastogne (26 Dec–2 Jan) which the Germans lost.

The fighting in Russia continued, but it was now the Soviet troops who were doing all the attacking.

1945

The Allied advance continued despite the Arnhem setback and troops crossed the Rhine in March, the German forces surrendering in May as British, American and Russian forces met in Berlin.

Japan capitulated later the same year after two atomic bombs were dropped on Hiroshima and Nagasaki.

In other theatres, smaller in scale but none the less important for that, fierce fighting took place.

The US forces in the Philippines and the Pacific fought an intense island-hopping war with the Japanese as each tiny atoll was contested. Names like Bataan, Corregidor, Guadalcanal, Iwo Jima and Okinawa spring to mind as the US units finally ousted the fanatical Japanese troops from their positions.

In Burma and Malaya, British and Japanese troops clashed in a jungle war. Singapore fell in 1942, but General Slim had recaptured Burma by March 1945 in a campaign that is surely a classic military operation.

No mention has so far been made of the air and sea struggles which played key parts in the war. Without the support of the Royal Air Force and Royal Navy, the Normandy invasion could not have taken place. The US forces in the Pacific could not have carried out their grim task so successfully had it not been for the support of their Naval forces and carrier-based aircraft.

All three arms combined to produce an effective battle machine so vast that only limited aspects of the war can ever be recreated on the wargames table.

Simple Wargame Rules for World War 2
Movement: Infantry 6″
Lorries 12″
Armoured cars 15″

	Tanks 10"
	Field Artillery 3"
Firing:	Rifle 24"
	Sub machine gun 12"
	Light machine gun 24"
	Heavy machine gun 36"
	Mortars 12"-36" (cannot fire at less than 12")
	Tank gun (including anti tank) 60"
	Field gun 72"

Firing:

Tanks 10"
Field Artillery 3"
Rifle 24"
Sub machine gun 12"
Light machine gun 24"
Heavy machine gun 36"
Mortars 12"-36" (cannot fire at less than 12")
Tank gun (including anti tank) 60"
Field gun 72"

Rifle fire: One dice per figure, '5' or '6' kills, '4-6' under half range.

Machine guns: Three dice per weapon, score counting as casualties, halved at over half range (NB tanks often mounted varying numbers of machine guns, so these rules may apply to tank firing also).

Mortars: Minimum range 12", maximum 36". One dice thrown for target location: '5' or '6' on target, '4' bomb lands 2" to right of target, '3' 2" to left, '2' 2" over and '1' 2" short. One dice for effect, casualties as scored, no deductions.

Field & Tank guns: Two dice per gun, dice score casualties, halved over half range.

Anti-tank firing: Two dice per gun, '11-12' tank knocked out, '9-10' disabled for one turn, less than '9' no effect.

Field & Tank gun firing on lorries etc: Two dice per gun, '10-12' target destroyed, '8-9' disabled for one turn, less than '8' no effect.

Melees: Not really relevant, but if necessary one dice per eligible figure, highest score wins.

Suggested Reading

Barker A., *Panzers At War* (Ian Allan, 1978)

Blumenson M., *Rommel's Last Victory* (George Allen & Unwin, 1968)

Costello J., *The Pacific War* (Collins, 1981)

Davis B., *German Uniforms of the Third Reich* (Blandford, 1980)

Hapgood D. & Richardson D., *Monte Cassino* (Angus & Robertson, 1984)

Harris J., *Dunkirk* (David & Charles, 1980)

Hastings M., *Overlord* (Michael Joseph, 1984)

Larousse, *The Second World War* (Hamlyn, 1985)

Preston P., *The Spanish Civil War* (Weidenfeld & Nicolson, 1986)

Shachtman T., *The Phony War 1939–1940* (Harper & Row, 1982)
Sims J., *Arnhem Spearhead* (Imperial War Museum, 1978)
Spencer J., *Battle for Crete* (White Lion Publishing, 1976)
Thomas H., *The Spanish Civil War* (Eyre & Spottiswoode, 1961)
Urquhart R., *Arnhem* (Pan, 1960)
US Army, *Handbook of the Italian Army 1943* (Athena Books, 1983)
Windrow M., *The Waffen SS* (Osprey, 1982)
Wise T., *D-Day to Berlin* (A & AP, 1979)
Wise T., *World War 2 Military Vehicle Markings* (PSL, 1981)

The Modern Period, 1945–Present Day

Since the end of the Second World War there have been numerous smaller wars and minor actions, each more technically complex than its predecessor.

Air power has become an essential aspect of warfare. Aeroplanes now operate in multiple combat roles and continue to become more efficient in both hitting the enemy and avoiding his defences and countermeasures. The weapons carried by aircraft continue to become even more sophisticated as newer and newer technology becomes available.

Missiles, both air and ground launched, have also become important factors on the modern battlefield. Even the infantryman has his own personal missile defence on which to draw, in the shape of Milan and other systems. Most anti-aircraft systems are now missile orientated and the chief weapon of the aeroplane is often missiles.

The helicopter has become indispensable as a multi-purpose weapon on the modern battlefield. Usable for transport, observation, as a gun platform, for casualty evacuation, assault or whichever mode is required, this highly mobile machine has proved its worth in many wars, notably Vietnam.

As examples of conflicts since World War Two, we shall here briefly look at six minor wars. It should perhaps be underlined that the word minor is used in the sense of geographical limitations, rather than being dismissive of the actual conflict.

Indo China 1945–54

By 1945 the Communist Viet Minh guerrillas held much of North Vietnam and declared their independence. France, however, had formerly controlled the area as one of her colonies and was eager to re-establish French control.

A series of actions, notably the siege of Dienbienphu where

15,000 French soldiers held out from 20 November 1953 to 7 May 1954 before surrendering, saw the end of French control in Indo China.

The Korean War 1950–53

Communist North Korea, possessing a large, well-trained and Russian-equipped army, invaded South Korea in June 1950. The army of the Republic of Korea was hardly more than a police force and South Korea asked the recently formed United Nations for help. The United Nations responded by sending in troops – mostly American – and after a series of actions the armistice saw the boundary line established to the satisfaction of both North and South Korea.

The Korean war was the first major war to take place in what was now the nuclear age. Nuclear weapons were not used, but their very existence was a factor during the conflict.

The Suez Crisis 1956

In July 1956 Egypt took control of the Suez Canal (which connects the Red and Mediterranean Seas) from the mainly British corporation who ran it. The British Government, aided by the French, sent in armed forces in the following November.

British paratroopers landed on Port Said at the northern end of the canal, while British and French warships bombarded the town. The bombardment was followed by a landing of troops who quickly captured the town and advanced inland. The United

American troops in action. Infantrymen scrounge a lift on an M113 vehicle, all courtesy of Platoon 20. (Photo Model Figures & Hobbies)

Nations demanded a ceasefire and sent in troops from ten nations to supervise the cessation of hostilities.

The Six Day War 1967

June 1967 saw the threat of another Arab invasion of Israel. Previous attempts had been made in 1948 and 1956 and on this third occasion Israel took the initiative and launched a pre-emptive attack. The Israeli air force destroyed a large part of the Egyptian air force on the ground and then turned its attention to Jordan and Syria to repeat the process. Supported by their planes, Israeli land forces struck the Arabs hard, using tactics which were both mobile and flexible.

Most of the fighting took place in Sinai and as the Israelis advanced, the Arab forces had no option but to fall back. The Israeli forces rode into Jerusalem and reached the Suez Canal, defeating the Jordanian and Arab forces en route. The remaining enemy, Syria, surrendered.

In six days Israel had fought a successful offensive on three fronts and suffered few casualties in the process.

Vietnam

In 1963 the South Vietnamese government was overthrown by a military coup. The following year the USA declared its support for South Vietnam in the face of aggression by the communist Viet Cong from the north. By 1965 America was mounting regular bombing raids against North Vietnam and it was in the same year that the first US Marines landed in the South.

The Tet Offensive in 1968 was a major Viet Cong attack against the South and pushed the South Vietnamese and the Americans back. By 1973 US troops were being withdrawn from the war, due to American public opinion and in 1975 the South Vietnamese forces surrendered, thus ending the conflict.

A fierce looking assortment of 20mm Viet Cong with a variety of weapons by Platoon 20. It was these troops which formed the bulk of the Communist forces during the Vietnam War. (Photo Model Figures & Hobbies)

The Falklands War 1982

In April 1982, Argentinian forces invaded the Falkland Islands, claiming them for Argentina.

Britain speedily launched a task force which arrived in the area later that month. By the end of April, South Georgia had been retaken and the task force turned its attention to the Falklands themselves.

A beach-head was established at San Carlos Water on East Falkland and British troops moved inland. After fierce actions at Goose Green, Mount Kent, Wireless Ridge, Mount Longdon and Two Sisters, British forces occupied positions which overlooked the capital, Port Stanley.

On 12 June the Argentinian forces in Port Stanley surrendered and the war was over.

Simple Wargame Rules for the Modern Period

Movement: Infantry 6"
Wheeled vehicles 15"
Tracked vehicles 12"

Firing: Rifle 36"
Sub machine guns 15"
Light machine guns 30"
Heavy machine guns 40"
Mortars 12"–40"
Tank Guns 60"
Field Guns 72"

NB: Tank and field guns may also be read as surface to surface missiles.

Rifle fire: One dice per figure, '5' or '6' kills, '4-6' under half range.

Machine guns: Three dice per weapon, score counting as casualties, halved at over half range.

Mortars: Minimum range 12", maximum 40". One dice thrown for target location: '5' or '6' on target, '4' bomb lands 2" to right of target, '3' 2" to left, '2' 2" over and '1' 2" short. One dice for effect, casualties as scored, no deductions.

Field and Tank guns (including surface to surface missiles): Two dice per gun, dice score casualties, halved at over half range.

Anti-Tank fire (including ground operated missile systems etc.): Two dice per gun. '11-12' target knocked out, '9-10' disabled for one turn, less than

An alternative for a modern wargame is the range of Afghans available from Platoon 20. This conflict offers a chance to pit what are basically natives against a highly mechanised modern army. (Photo Model Figures & Hobbies)

'9' no effect.

Field & Tank guns on lorries etc: Two dice per gun, '10-12' target knocked out, '8-9' disabled for one turn, less than '8' no effect.

Melees: Not really relevant, but if required, one dice per figure, highest score wins.

Suggested Reading

Barnaby F., *Future War* (Michael Joseph, 1985)

Berman R. & Gunston B., *Rockets & Missiles of World War III* (Bison Hamlyn, 1983)

Bonds R. (ed), *The Soviet War Machine* (Hamlyn, 1977)

Dewar M., *The British Army in Northern Ireland* (A & AP, 1985)

Dickens P., *SAS: The Jungle Frontier* (A & AP, 1983)

Hackett J., *The Third World War* (Sphere, 1979)

Hackett J., *The Untold Story* (Nel, 1983)

Hogg I., *The British Army of the 20th Century* (Ian Allan, 1985)

Katcher P., *Armies of the Vietnam War 1962–75* (Osprey, 1980)

Laffin J., *Fight for the Falklands* (Sphere, 1982)

Miller H., *Jungle War in Malaya* (A. Barker, 1972)

Morse S. (ed), *Modern Military Powers: Israel* (Temple Press, 1984)

Pimlott J. (ed), *The Middle East Conflicts* (Orbis, 1983)

Richardson D., *An Illustrated Guide to the Techniques and Equipment of Electronic Warfare* (Salamander, 1985)

Roy J., *The Battle of Dienbienphu* (Faber & Faber, 1965)

Sack J., *Bodycount* (Hutchinson, 1971)

Shaplen R., *The Road From War: Vietnam 1965–70* (Andre Deutsch, 1971)

Smith D., *The British Army 1965–80* (Osprey, 1977)

Sunday Times, *The Falklands War* (Andre Deutsch, 1982)

3 In closing

Research

The above period summaries and suggested rules have obviously been deliberately simplified as an aid to their speedy assimila-
tion by the reader.

Once the wargamer has decided on which period to recreate,
further research will be needed. The short book list at the end of
each chapter in section 2 will offer some immediate sources but
a few remarks on research may be beneficial here.

As mentioned above, once a period has been selected for
further investigation it is a good idea to purchase a folder or note
book. In this can be filed or written all the relevant information
which is discovered concerning the period in question. This
single item may be sufficient or perhaps the amassed data
outgrows it and a second file is needed. From small beginnings
are created quite bulky files – cross-referenced and indexed,
providing their owner with a valuable source of information.

The first port of call as one sets out to discover more about a
chosen period is the local library. If the required works are not
actually on the shelves, the library system means that they can
generally be obtained from another branch in a surprisingly
short time.

Notes can be taken from these books, but take great care not
to write on the book itself or mark it in any way.

Should you wish to purchase a book rather than loan it from a
library, then pay a visit to or get in touch with a reputable dealer
in military books. Such books often tend to hold their price, so be
sure that you really do want to buy the book before laying out
money perhaps unnecessarily. A concise library of useful,
specialised books can be built up by effective purchases.

Visits to museums can be extremely useful – there is nothing
to compare with seeing the genuine article in order to add
information to your file. Museum staff are generally pleased to
answer questions and offer extra information on the exhibits.

An example of seeing the real thing. This type of artillery was in use both at sea and behind coastal defences during the 18th and 19th centuries. Its length of service makes the piece an ideal wargames item. A visit secures details on construction, deployment etc. (Photo R. Bendall)

Rough notes and sketches can be made on the spot, but usually prior permission has to be obtained for taking photographs. Museums often have small shops which sell very reasonably priced picture postcards depicting exhibits and these are extremely cost-effective additions to the research file.

Millitary magazines such as *Military Modelling* are also useful. While each issue is informative in itself, a complete year's run of 12, in a binder with an index, forms a valuable work.

Historical societies, re-enactment societies and the larger wargame clubs often have their own house magazines which often feature interesting articles.

Visits to castles and battlefields can be informative, as can the excellent displays staged by the numerous re-enactment societies – all are potential sources of extra information for the file.

Gradually as the notes increase you will have a good base on which to build, organise and use a wargame of a particular period.

One final point. While a specific period is interesting to study, general works are also useful – a list of typical titles is included. Each covers a fair proportion of history and thus offers a more overall view of a particular period.

General Reading List

Barthorp M., *The Armies of Britain 1485–1980* (NAM, 1982)

Chandler D., *Atlas of Military Strategy* (A&AP, 1980)

Dupuy P. and Dupuy T., *The Encyclopedia of Military History* (Macdonald, 1970)

Fuller J., *Decisive Battles of the Western World* (2 Vols) (Paladin, 1970)

Humble R., *Famous Land Battles* (St Michael, 1980)

Keegan J. & Holmes R., *Soldiers* (Hamish Hamilton, 1981)

Koch H., *The Rise of Modern Warfare 1618–1815* (Hamlyn Bison, 1981)

Lawson C., *A History of Uniforms of the British Army* (5 Vols) (Kaye & Ward, 1967–9)

MacDonald J., *Great Battlefields of the World* (Michael Joseph 1984)

Schick I., (ed) *Battledress* (Peerage Books, 1983)

Figure Manufacturers

There now follows a fairly representative list of wargame figure manufacturers, along with an indication as to the size of figures produced. Bear in mind, however, that sizes of model soldiers do

A cardboard farm (of the correct period) cut out and assembled makes a very cost effective and useful item of wargames scenery.

An English Civil War colour party.

vary – the quoted 15mm can in fact be anywhere between 12 & 18mm. While the information was correct at the time the list was compiled, such information will inevitably date, but it is hoped that the bulk of the list will remain accurate for some time.

When writing to companies for further information, always enclose a self-addressed and stamped envelope, which will speed up a reply.

Battle Honours
(15mm)

Samuel Cottage
5 Moors Lane
Oreton
Nr Cleobury Mortimer
Kidderminster
Worcs DY14 8RH

Britannia Miniatures
(25mm)

33 St Mary's Road
Halton Village
Runcorn
Cheshire WA7 2BJ

Dixon Miniatures
(15 & 25mm)

Unit 28, Spring Grove Mills
Linthwaite
Huddersfield
West Yorkshire

Donnington Miniatures
(15mm)

15 Cromwell Rd
Shaw
Newbury
Berkshire

Essex Miniatures
(15 & 25mm)

Unit 1, Shannon Centre
Shannon Square
Thames Estuary Estate
Canvey Island
Essex SS8 0PE

Frei Korps
(15mm)

25 Princetown Road
Bangor
Co Down
BT20 3TA N. Ireland

Frontier Miniatures
(25 & 15mm)

7343 Branding Iron
Canutillo
Texas 79835 USA

Gallia Reproductions
(15mm)

35 Clough Road
Gosberton, Risegate
Spalding, Lincs
Lincs

Harrow Model Shop
(20 & 25mm)

190–194 Station Road
Harrow
Middlesex

Heroes Miniatures
(20mm)

7 Waverley Place
Worksop
Nottinghamshire

Contrast in sizes. 6, 15 and 20mm figures compared. Surprising, isn't it?

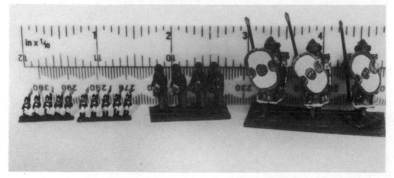

Unusual size – 40mm – British and American WW1 and WW2 figures from Spanish maker Taxdir Miniatures.

Heroic & Ros Figures
(15 & 6mm)

Unit 12, Semington Turnpike
Semington
Trowbridge
Wiltshire BA14 6LB

Hovels With Campaigns Ltd (25 & 15mm)

18 Glebe Road
Scartho
Grimsby
South Humberside DN33 2HL

Irregular Miniatures
(25 & 6mm)

18 The Avenue
Norton
Malton
North Yorkshire YO17 9EF

Miniature Figurines Ltd
(25 & 15mm)

1–5 Graham Road
Southampton
SO2 0AX

Standard bearers and Ironside troopers, English Civil War, from Western Miniatures.

Model Figures & Hobbies
(20mm)

Lower Balloo Road
Groomsport
Co Down
BT19 2LU N. Ireland

Peter Laing
(15mm)

Minden
Sutton St Nicholas
Hereford HR1 3BD

Pioneer Miniatures
(15mm)

15 Mount Pleasant
Brierley Hill
West Midlands

Q.T. Models
(25mm)

17 Hilderthorpe Road
Bridlington
N. Humberside YO15 3AY

RSM Ltd
(25 & 20mm)

513 E. Maxwell St
Lexington
Kentucky 40508 USA

SKT Wargame Figures
(25 & 15mm)

9 Wargrave Road
Twyford
Berkshire

Skylrex Ltd
(25 & 20mm)

28 Brook Street
Wymeswold
Loughborough
Leicestershire

Zulu warriors and weapons in plastic from Esci.

Siege tower accessory from Premier Products for siege games.

Spencer Smith Miniatures
(30mm)

88 Greencroft Gdns
London NW6 3JQ

Tabletop Games
(25 & 15mm)

53 Mansfield Road
Daybrook
Nottingham NG5 6BB

Tradition
(30 & 25mm)

5A Shepherd Street
Mayfair
London W1

Wargames Foundry
(25mm)

21 Villiers Road
Woodthorpe
Nottingham NG5 4FB

Warrior Miniatures
(25 & 15mm)

14 Tiverton Avenue
Glasgow
G32 9NX

Research will turn up chronicles of smaller wars and unusual actions.
This diorama of an 'Attack on Gate Pa' shows British troops in conflict
with Maoris and is the sort of incident which could make an interesting
and different wargame.

Wargaming Library

Finally there follows a comprehensive list of all the wargaming titles published. Most are now out of print but can still be obtained via the public library system or from a reputable dealer in military books.

Wargames Bibliography

Asquith S.A., *The Campaign of Naseby 1645* (Osprey Wargames No. 1, 1979)

Barker P., *Ancient Wargaming. Airfix Magazine Guide 9* (Patrick Stephens Ltd., 1975)

———, *Know The Game: Wargaming* (EP Publishing Ltd., 1976)

Bath T., *Setting Up a Wargames Campaign* (Wargames Research Group 1973, 1987)

Carter B., *Naval Wargames: World War I & World War II* (David & Charles, 1975)

Dunn P., *Sea Battles* (MAP 1970)

Featherstone D.F., *Advanced War Games* (Stanley Paul, 1969)

———, *Air Wargames* (Stanley Paul, 1966)

———, *Battle Notes for Wargamers* (David & Charles, 1973)

———, *Battles With Model Soldiers* (David & Charles, 1970)

———, *Naval Wargames* (Stanley Paul, 1965)

———, *Skirmish Wargaming* (Patrick Stephens Ltd, 1975)

———, *Solo-Wargaming* (Kaye & Ward, 1973)

———, *Tackle Model Soldiers This Way* (Stanley Paul, 1963)

———, *Tank Battles In Miniature* (Series): Vol 1 Western Desert 1940–42 (Patrick Stephens Ltd, 1973); Vol 4 Mediterranean Campaigns 1943–45 (Patrick Stephens Ltd, 1977)

———, *War Game Campaigns* (Stanley Paul, 1970)

———, *War Games* (Stanley Paul, 1962)

———, *Wargames Through the Ages* (Series): Vol 1 3000BC–1500AD (Stanley Paul, 1972); Vol 2 1420–1783 (Stanley Paul, 1974); Vol 3 1792–1859 (Stanley Paul, 1975); Vol 4 1861–1945 (Stanley Paul, 1976)

———, *Wargamers Handbook Of The American War of Independence 1775–1783* (MAP, 1977)

———, *Wargaming Ancient & Medieval Periods* (David & Charles, 1975)

———, *Wargaming Airborne Operations* (Kaye & Ward, 1977)

———, *Wargaming Pike and Shot* (David & Charles, 1977)

Featherstone D.F. and Robinson K., *Battles with Model Tanks* (Macdonald & Janes, 1979)

Galloway B. (Ed) *Fantasy Wargaming* (Patrick Stephens Ltd, 1981)

Grant C., *Ancient Battles For Wargamers* (Argus Books, 1977)

———, *Ancient Wargame, The* (A & C Black, 1974)

———, *Battle! Practical Wargaming* (MAP, 1970)

———, *Napoleonic Wargaming* (MAP, 1974)

———, *War Game, The* (A & C Black, 1971)

———, *Wargame Tactics* (Cassell, 1979)

Grant C.S., *Programmed Wargames Scenarios* (WRG)

———, *Scenarios For Wargames* (WRG, 1983)

Griffith P., *Napoleonic Wargaming For Fun* (Ward Lock, 1980)

Gush G. with Finch A., *A Guide To Wargaming* (Croom Helm, 1980)

Gush G. and Windrow A., *English Civil War, The* Airfix Magazine Guide 28 (Patrick Stephens Ltd, 1978)

Hague P., *Sea Battles In Miniature: A Guide To Naval Wargaming* (Patrick Stephens Ltd, 1980)

Heath I., *A Wargamer's Guide To The Crusades* (Patrick Stephens Ltd, 1980)

Holmes J., *Fantasy Role Playing Games* (A & AP, 1981)

Jeffrey G., *The Napoleonic Wargame* (Almark, 1974)

Livingstone I., *Dicing With Dragons* (Routledge, Keegan Paul, 1982)

Lyall G. *Operation Warboard* (A & C Black, 1977)

Morschauser J., *How To Play Wargames In Miniature* (Walker & Co, 1962)

Nash D., *Wargames* (Hamlyn, 1974)

Parker J., *The Campaign Of Leipzig 1813* (Osprey Wargames No. 2, 1979)

Perry F., *First Book of Wargaming, A* (Argus Books, 1977)

———, *Second Book of Wargaming, The* (Argus Books, 1978)

Quarrie B., *Napoleon's Campaigns In Miniature: A Wargamers Guide to the Napoleonic Wars 1796–1815* (Patrick Stephens Ltd, 1977)

———, (Ed) *PSL Guide to Wargaming* (Patrick Stephens Ltd, 1980)

———, *Tank Battles In Miniature* (Series): Vol 2 Russian Campaign 1941–45 (Patrick Stephens Ltd, 1975); Vol 3 North West European Campaign 1944–45 (Patrick Stephens Ltd, 1976); Vol 5 Arab-Israeli Wars (Patrick Stephens Ltd, 1978)

———, *World War 2 Wargaming* Airfix Magazine Guide 15 (Patrick Stephens Ltd, 1976)

Reisswitz Von, *Kriegsspiel 1824* (Bill Leeson, 1981)

Sanders J., *An Introduction To Wargaming* (Pelham Books Ltd, 1976)

Spick M., *Air Battles in Miniature* (Patrick Stephens Ltd, 1978)

Taylor A., *Rules For Wargaming* (Shire Publications Ltd, 1971)

Tunstill J., (Ed) *Discovering English Civil Wargaming* (Shire Publications Ltd, 1973)

———, *Discovering Wargames* (Shire Publications Ltd, 1973)

Wells H.G., *Little Wars* (Arms & Armour Press, 1970 reprint)

Wesencraft C., *Practical Wargaming* (The Elmfield Press, 1974)

———, *With Pike And Musket* (The Elmfield Press, 1975)

Wilson A., *War Gaming* (Penguin, 1970)

Wise T., *American Civil War Wargaming* Airfix Magazine Guide 4 (Patrick Stephens Ltd, 1977)

———, *Battles for Wargamers* (Series): American Civil War 1862, The (MAP, 1972); Peninsular War: 1813 (MAP, 1974); Roman Civil Wars 49–45BC (MAP, 1974); World War II: Tunisia (MAP, 1973); World War II: The Western Desert (MAP, 1972); 2nd Punic War, The (MAP, 1972)

———, *Introduction To Battle Gaming* (MAP, 1969)

Young P. (Ed) *The War Game* (Cassel, 1972)

Young P. & Lawford J., *Charge! Or How To Play Wargames* (Morgan Grampian, 1967, reprint Athena Wargames Library, 1986)

My thanks are due to Terry Wise of Athena Books (34, Imperial Crescent, Town Moor, Doncaster, South Yorkshire DN2 5BU) for all his assistance in compiling this bibliography.

TAILPIECE

I hope you have found this book both useful and interesting. Inevitably, there will still be some unanswered queries and points which require further explanation and clarification.

If you write to me at the following address:

> c/o The Editor
> Military Modelling Magazine
> ASP Ltd
> Wolsey House
> Wolsey Road
> Hemel Hempstead
> Hertfordshire HP2 4SS

enclosing an SAE, I will do my best to answer your questions.

Happy Wargaming!

INDEX

MAKE SURE

MILITARY
MODELLING

REPORTS FOR ACTION TO YOU EVERY MONTH
BECOME A SUBSCRIBER TODAY

£16.90 for 12 issues U.K.
£21.00 for 12 issues Overseas Surface Mail
£48.00 for 12 issues Overseas Air Mail

If you would like to subscribe to Military Modelling please make
your cheque, postal order or international money order payable
to ARGUS SPECIALIST PUBLICATIONS LTD, or send your
Access/Barclaycard number to the following address or
telephone your credit card order on 0442 48432

Send your remittance to:
INFONET LTD., Times House,
179 The Marlowes, Hemel Hempstead,
Herts. HP1 1BB.